A Southern Woman's Story

AMERICAN CIVIL WAR CLASSICS
Gary W. Gallagher and Robert K. Krick

A Memoir of the Last Year of the War
for Independence in the Confederate States of America
Jubal A. Early
with a new introduction by
Gary W. Gallagher

A Southern Woman's Story
Phoebe Yates Pember
with a new introduction by
George C. Rable

A Southern Woman's Story

Phoebe Yates Pember

with a new introduction by
George C. Rable

University of South Carolina Press

© 2002 University of South Carolina

Published in Columbia, South Carolina, by the
University of South Carolina Press

Manufactured in the United States of America

06 05 04 03 02   5 4 3 2 1

Library of Congress Cataloging-in-Publication Data

Pember, Phoebe Yates, 1823–1913.
    A Southern woman's story / Phoebe Yates Pember ; with a new introduction by George C.
Rable.
        p. cm. — (American Civil War classics)
    Originally published: New York : G.W. Carleton & Co. ; London : S. Low, Son & Co., 1879.
ISBN 1-57003-451-6 (alk. paper)
    1. Pember, Phoebe Yates, 1823–1913. 2. United States—History—Civil War, 1861–1865—
Personal narratives, Confederate. 3. Richmond (Va.)—History—Civil War, 1861–1865—
Personal narratives, Confederate. 4. United States—History—Civil War, 1861–1865—
Hospitals. 5. Chimborazo Hospital (Richmond, Va.) 6. United States—History—Civil War,
1861–1865—Medical care. 7. Medicine, Military—Confederate States of America—History. 8.
Hospitals—Confederate States of America—Staff—Biography. 9. Women—Confederate States
of America—Biography. I. Title. II. Series.
E625 .P39 2002
973.7'82—dc21   2001057957

CONTENTS

Series Editors' Preface

The generation that watched escalating sectional tensions explode into violent conflict in 1861 created an imposing published record. A struggle that killed more than 600,000 soldiers, subjected untold numbers of civilians to cruel material and emotional stress, and wrought enormous social and political changes prompted many individuals to chronicle their experiences. Such witnesses have much to teach modern readers, who can look to American Civil War Classics for paperback editions of important firsthand accounts. The series will cast a wide net, presenting testimony from men and women—both soldiers and civilians—in the United States and the Confederacy. It will present different types of works, including sets of letters and diaries written as the war unfolded as well as memoirs and reminiscences penned from a retrospective vantage point. Historians of the period will introduce the titles, placing them within the war's rich historiography and providing details about their authors. The volumes should appeal to both scholars and lay readers interested in inexpensive editions of essential texts.

Phoebe Yates Pember's *A Southern Woman's Story*, the second title in the series, ranks among the most cited books on the Confederate home front. It abounds with information about medical care for Confederate soldiers, the ways in which the war thrust women into public roles, day-to-day life amid growing hardship in the Southern capital, and a range of other topics. Introduced by George C. Rable, the author of a prize-winning study of Confederate women, *A Southern Woman's Story* affords an opportunity to view the war as described and analyzed by a person of intelligence, whose eye for the telling story enlivens a most revealing narrative.

GARY W. GALLAGER
ROBERT K. KRICK

Editor's Introduction

Phoebe Yates Pember, the fourth of seven children, was born into a prominent Charleston family in 1823. Her father, Jacob Clavius Levy, a successful businessman with substantial railroad and insurance interests, had met Phoebe's mother, Fanny Yates, while visiting Liverpool. This devout Jewish family lived on fashionable East Bay Street and worshiped at nearby Kahal Kadosh Beth Elohim. Although little is known about Pember's early years or education, her writings and letters reveal considerable literary sophistication, and Robert Rosen has suggested that she may have attended a northern finishing school.[1]

In 1856 Phoebe married a Christian, Thomas Pember. How her family reacted to this choice is unknown, and whether it contributed to later problems in Phoebe's family is equally unclear. For a time the couple lived in Boston, Massachusetts, but Thomas fell ill with tuberculosis and in July 1861 died at Aiken, South Carolina. Phoebe Pember then lived with her family, who were refugees in Marietta, Georgia—an arrangement that proved extremely trying and difficult for all involved.

In late 1862, with the encouragement of Mary Elizabeth Adams Randolph, the wife of Secretary of War George Randolph, the thirty-nine-year-old Pember become a chief matron in the massive Chimborazo Hospital in Richmond, Virginia. However pleased she may have been to escape the tense family situation in Marietta, she had exchanged one set of troubles for another. Pember entered an environment that many Confederates (and Americans generally), regardless of gender, considered unsuitable for women. Perhaps even more significantly, she had to wrestle with the complexities of management and supply that presented a microcosm of the beleaguered Confederacy's chronic, and in the end insurmountable, problems.

Chimborazo was a sprawling complex that served approximately 76,000 patients during the war. Hospital officials resented what several termed the arrival of "petticoat government" (3), but Pember's competence, efficiency, and tenacity soon won her respect from the chief surgeon and other doctors without ever entirely overcoming resistance to her no-nonsense approach to administration. Despite the sometimes heated nature of the bureaucratic battles, in her memoir Pember presents a remarkably fair-minded portrait of doctors, and in fact her description of other women is often far more critical and biting. Personal friction, however, was only part of the challenge. Pember's memoir indirectly shows how critical the whole nature of complex organizations remained to the conduct of the Civil War. Pember had to maneuver her way carefully through a maze of surgeons and assistant surgeons. In several respects her story becomes a tale of progress as she brings system and order to a chaotic world. Confusion often reigned: for example, it was only after several weeks at Chimborazo that she learned from a doctor that she could delegate cooking chores to attendants. And even as Pember quickly mastered the job, the scope of her authority remained in doubt. A case in point was the continuous struggle for control of the "whiskey barrel." Too often the apothecary and his clerks drained the contents before the patients had received their medicinal portions, and one intoxicated surgeon actually set the wrong leg of a badly injured soldier. Pember finally insisted that the whiskey be locked up in her pantry, but bitter resentment against this policy persisted throughout much of her tenure. Quarts of whiskey set aside for nighttime "emergencies" were almost always empty by morning. But however frustrating these problems became, Pember stood her ground against drunken ward-masters and surgeons.

Pember at first assumed that employing women might ease such difficulties, yet one assistant matron became so drunk and belligerent that she finally had to be carried out of the ward. A series of confrontations with women who either were inept or offended by the chief matron's supposed aloofness left Pember increasingly isolated. She later confessed to considerable uncertainty about whether to employ "ladies of education and position" or women from the "common class of respectable servants" (18), though she eventually decided that the presence of refined "ladies" greatly improved care.

A steady stream of visitors also hampered Pember's efforts to run the wards efficiently. Marylanders and Virginians trooped to the hospital, some virtually camping out to be near convalescent soldiers. One especially persistent family set up housekeeping in the ward and refused to leave until Pember finally handed one wounded soldier a new shirt and pair of drawers, telling him to put them on after she departed. The impudent family still ended up sleeping in Pember's laundry room for nearly a week. The patient eventually recovered but was later wounded and brought back to Chimborazo. His annoying wife reappeared and later gave birth to a baby right in the ward.

The frustrations and drudgery of hospital life never quite suppressed Pember's desire to cut a figure in society and in some ways exacerbated her social prejudices. She complained of a "great many inefficient and uneducated women, hardly above the laboring classes" (1) who sought hospital work, yet she also portrayed the women of the South generally as sturdy patriots always ready to make sacrifices for the humblest Confederate soldier. According to Pember, as late as the spring of 1864, many women remained fearless in the face of invasion and hardship. Ironically, however, Pember's own account undermines her efforts to portray Confederates as stalwart, noble, and unified. Ungrammatical notes from grousing surgeons appalled her because she was "accustomed to be treated with extreme deference and courtesy by the highest officials connected with the gover[n]ment" (12). And until almost the eve of Richmond's fall, Pember hobnobbed with the capital's elite, eagerly devouring the latest fashion news from Baltimore.[2] At times she recognized her own anomalous attitudes and recoiled from the capital's decadence; and in an early 1864 letter she sternly remarked: "If Spartan austerity is to win our independence, we are a lost nation. I do not like the signs, and fear the writing on the wall."[3]

Such comments were not necessarily unusual among women of Pember's class and probably reflected her growing appreciation of how so many ordinary people were suffering and dying for the Confederate cause. Indeed, one of the great virtues of her memoir is the sympathetic treatment of ordinary soldiers. Her stories of hospital life give voice to illiterate men whose feelings, thoughts, and experiences have generally been lost to history. Although she could condescendingly write about a soldier who "like all the humbler class of men . . . think that unless they have been living on hog and hominy they are starved" (6), she more often described patients with both sympathy and humor. Her eye for detail and ear for dialogue were occasionally reminiscent of Charles Dickens. When offered some soup, one poor fellow "took a piece of well-masticated tobacco from between three or four solitary teeth." He then reached under his pillow for a religious tract, tearing off a page to wipe his nose. "My mammy's soup was not like that," he declared, but he thought he might "worry a little down if it war'n't for them *weeds* [parsley] a-floating round" (7). Pember grew to understand soldiers who rejected various foods prescribed by surgeons, and recognized that some men simply refused to eat in the hopes they might be granted a furlough.

Of course, Pember could mindlessly repeat common stereotypes, such as a story about a dying Irishmen who preferred whiskey to religious consolation. She never escaped a tendency to treat illiterate soldiers as simple children, but most of her accounts also exude a warm, human sympathy and reveal a toleration for patients who perhaps were not quite so forlorn as they pretended. At the same time, the limits of Pember's own social vision become apparent. She notes that for most soldiers "gratitude" was a new and somewhat disturbing idea. She came to believe that thankfulness had to be cultivated, but she also recognized that many men hesitated to show their appreciation for fear that it might obligate them somehow to reciprocate any help or kindness. Her patients were in fact starving not only for food but also for attention. One especially pathetic fellow did not want his nails cut because he used them like a spoon, and refused to allow his hair to be trimmed because he had promised his mother to let his unruly locks grow until the war was over. When he haltingly tried to dictate a letter home, Pember began asking him questions about his experiences and soon filled up four pages. In utter amazement, the soldier asked Pember if she was married, and when told she was a widow, he archly commented, "You wait!" (15).

Aside from vivid descriptions, Pember portrays her charges with a remarkable realism. One mortally wounded Marylander wanted his widowed mother to know that he had "died in what I consider the defense of civil rights and liberties." Yet he quickly added, "I may be wrong. God alone knows" (25). Pember sometimes portrays patients as uncomplaining paragons, bluff heroes who could joke about whether their sweethearts would refuse to kiss them after seeing their disfiguring wounds, but then also notes their irritating habits or describes how maggots swarmed and wounds stank. Even though *A Southern Woman's Story* contains its share of stock deathbed scenes, it also mentions the soldiers who simply wasted away from "nostalgia," or what we would call homesickness.

The evolution of Pember's own attitudes reflected larger changes in the Confederacy. When she was first approached about taking a position at Chimborazo, the thought that "such a life would be injurious to the delicacy and refinement of a lady" (2) immediately crossed Pember's mind. The demands of the work, however, soon drove away such thoughts, and like soldiers who had witnessed great suffering on the battlefields, she grew accustomed if not hardened to the sight of corpses. When summoned by a dying patient, she marveled at having "no timidity and hardly any sensibility left."[4] She had learned how to close a dead man's eyes and then quickly resume her rounds. Pember, however, recognized that many of her fellow Southerners might still have doubts about whether a woman's delicacy could survive such experiences. At the end of her memoir, she tactfully notes that "there is no unpleasant exposure under proper arrangements," and even when there is, a "woman *must* soar beyond the conventional modesty considered correct under different circumstances" (90). This seems a flat and rather peculiar conclusion to the memoir, but unlike nurses such as Kate Cumming who railed against their countrywomen for shirking their duties in the hospitals, Pember seldom raises any controversial questions.

Oftentimes in her writing, Pember seems satisfied with simply cataloging hospital conditions. Although shortages and inflation had plagued both doctors and nurses from the beginning of the war, by the bloody battle summer of 1864, many patients were subsisting on small, dry pieces of corn-bread—much like their comrades in the field. The ever-present rats, often discussed with a kind of wry humor, became sources of frustration and eventually of food. Pember adds that Yankee prisoners received the same half-rations as Southern soldiers, and like many Confederates, she sounds especially defensive on this question, at one point sharply noting the skeleton-like appearance of prisoners returning from Northern camps.

The whole idea of hardship, presented in sometimes graphic detail, becomes an important theme of *A Southern Woman's Story*. Aside from the expected shortages of food, readers learn a great deal about a nurse's living conditions. For a time, Pember stayed in a whitewashed board house on the hospital grounds that also served as kitchen and laundry. During the winter, as wind whipped through crevices in the walls, she rested on a straw pallet in the center of a room. She fared little better renting cramped, over-priced rooms in the city. At one point, she spent two weeks in bed with rheumatism, later noting that a combination of heat and exposure to men with typhoid might have caused some unspecified illness. In one war-time letter, Pember admitted badly needing the income from her hospital work and candidly remarked, "Who would suppose or believe that days passed among fever wards and dying men . . . with no comforts and every privation was voluntary!"[5] As for the patients themselves, they often received crudely sewn clothing from home—in itself a rough index of hard times. Between troubles with shortages and patients, Pember herself grew increasingly exhausted, and her frustrations in many ways mirrored those of her society.[6]

For example, sectional divisions within the Confederacy cropped up even in the hospitals. Virginians scorned Marylanders and vice versa. Eventually patients were segregated by state; officers occupied their own wards. Echoes of internal conflict from various parts of the Confederacy reverberated through the buildings. Patients received letters from home describing terrible hardships, and according to Pember, these missives greatly contributed to desertion. During a leave of absence in October 1864, Pember endured an uncomfortable and interrupted rail journey that must have set her to thinking about how much longer the Confederate transportation system, if such it could be called, would hold together.

Returning to Chimborazo, Pember witnessed the Southern nation's final days. The collapse of the Confederate defenses came suddenly, and she recounts how some civilians carried off commissary supplies while others scrambled to leave Richmond. The fires, explosion, and sheer chaos are nicely recaptured in paragraphs filled with interesting detail. And unlike many other accounts, Pember's goes on to tell the story of Union occupation, continued hardships, and general ennui. Her last-ditch defense of the whiskey barrel against thirsty looters almost anticipates twentieth-century descriptions of war's bureaucratic absurdities.

Like her sharp-tongued sister Eugenia Phillips, who was imprisoned by the infamous Union general Benjamin F. Butler, Phoebe Pember remained a staunch Confederate patriot throughout the war. Did her persistent fortitude reflect personal self-confidence or did it have deeper origins? One might speculate, for example, about what impact marrying a Christian had on her religious faith. There is no evidence that she converted, and Robert

Rosen has argued persuasively that she remained loyal to Judaism. Nevertheless, at one point Pember sadly remarks about the Confederacy's final months: "When we review the past, it would seem that Christianity was but a name—that the Atonement had failed, and Christ had lived and died in vain" (56). Yet this admittedly isolated and cryptic remark is the only bit of information that casts doubt on Pember's religious convictions.[7]

Whatever the exact nature of her own faith, she perceptively notes how the devout could hold especially ferocious attitudes toward their country's enemies. In a letter written in September 1863, Pember effectively recaptures the intensity of wartime hatred: "The feeling here against the Yankees exceeds anything I could imagine, particularly among the good Christians. I spent an evening among a particularly pious sett [*sic*]. One lady said she had a pile of Yankee bones lying around her pump so that the first glance on opening her eyes would rest upon them. Another begged me to get her a Yankee Skull to keep her toilette trinkets in." Unable to remain silent, Pember at last "lifted my voice and congratulated myself at being born of a nation, and religion that did not enjoin forgiveness on its enemies, that enjoyed the blessed privilege of praying for an eye for an eye, and a life for a life, and was not one of those for whom Christ died in vain." She then jocosely suggested these Christians should "all join the Jewish Church, let forgiveness and peace and good will alone and put their trust in the sword of the Lord and Gideon."[8] And indeed, Pember's own devotion to the Confederate cause often equaled the fervor she so perceptively analyzes here.

Unfortunately, information on Pember's life after the war is sketchy. She spent some time traveling, including four years in Europe near the end of the century, and wrote sketches and stories for popular magazines. On 4 March 1913, Phoebe Pember died in Pittsburgh, Pennsylvania, and was later buried at Laurel Grove Cemetery in Savannah, Georgia.

A Southern Woman's Story has obviously been Pember's most enduring legacy.[9] Pember began writing her account of hospital service almost immediately after the war. Thomas Cooper DeLeon arranged to have the work serialized in the first four issues of the newly established *Cosmopolite* magazine.[10] By the beginning of 1866, Pember had largely completed her memoir. She later changed a few words, made the dialogue with soldiers sound more colloquial, and included a small amount of information likely culled from postwar conversations. On a few occasions, she deleted or muted certain hostile and emotional sectional remarks. Otherwise, the book that was published by G. W. Carlton Company in New York and London in 1879 retains the fresh immediacy of a work composed shortly after the events being described. In his 1959 edition Bell Irvin Wiley divided the work into chapters, broke up long paragraphs, and also added nine of Pember's wartime letters.[11] The text of this American Civil War Classic edition is based upon the 1879 Carlton edition.

A Southern Woman's Story has become a classic Confederate memoir praised by historians and certainly an essential text for the study of Confederate medical history. Scholars have often ransacked Pember's memoirs and letters for quotations and anecdotes about wartime Richmond or Confederate nursing but more recently have also used Pember's insights to explore the complexities of women's lives in the wartime South.[12] Pember's stalwart Confederate nationalism undoubtedly makes her account less interesting to historians wishing to emphasize the waning of Confederate will, but most readers will enjoy her lively prose, fascinating stories, and insightful commentary on a range of subjects. In short, *A Southern Woman's Story* remains an important source of information in southern and Civil War history.

The author thanks Robert E. L. Krick of the Richmond National Battlefield Park for sharing his quite useful file of Pember materials.

A Southern Woman's Story

INTRODUCTION
Women of the South

Soon after the breaking out of the Southern war, the need of hospitals, properly organized and arranged, began to be felt, and buildings adapted for the purpose were secured by government. Richmond, being nearest the scene of action, took the lead in this matter, and the formerly hastily contrived accommodations for the sick were soon replaced by larger, more comfortable and better ventilated buildings.

The expense of keeping up small hospitals had forced itself upon the attention of the surgeon general, [Samuel P.] Moore, who on that account gradually incorporated them into half-a-dozen immense establishments, strewn around the suburbs. These were called Camp Jackson, Camp Winder, Chimborazo Hospital, Stuart Hospital and Howard Grove; and were arranged so that from thirty to forty wards formed a division, and generally five divisions a hospital. Each ward accommodated from thirty to forty patients, according to the immediate need for space. Besides the sick wards, similar buildings were used for official purposes, for in these immense establishments every necessary trade was carried on. There were the carpenter's, blacksmith's, apothecary's and shoemaker's shops; the ice-houses, commissary's and quartermaster's departments; and offices for surgeons, stewards, baggagemasters and clerks. Each division was furnished with all these, and each hospital presented to the eye the appearance of a small village.

There was no reason why, with this preparation for the wounded and sick, that they should not have received all the benefit of good nursing and food; but soon rumors began to circulate that there was something wrong in hospital administration, and Congress, desirous of remedying omissions, passed a law by which matrons were appointed. They had no official recognition, ranking even below stewards from a military point of view. Their pay was almost nominal from the depreciated nature of the currency. There had been a great deal of desultory visiting and nursing, by the women, previous to this law taking effect, resulting in more harm than benefit to the patients; and now that the field was open, a few, very few ladies, and a great many inefficient and uneducated women, hardly above the laboring classes, applied for and filled the offices.

The women of the South had been openly and violently rebellious from the moment they thought their states' rights touched. They incited the men to struggle in support of their views, and whether right or wrong, sustained them nobly to the end. They were the first to rebel—the last to succumb. Taking an active part in all that came within their sphere, and often compelled to go beyond this when the field demanded as many soldiers as could be raised; feeling a passion of interest in every man in the gray uniform of the Confederate service; they were doubly anxious to give comfort and assistance to the sick and wounded. In the course of a long and harassing war, with ports blockaded and harvests burnt, rail tracks constantly torn up, so that supplies of food were cut off, and sold always at exorbitant prices, no appeal was ever made to the women of the South, individually or collectively, that did not meet with a ready response. There was no parade of generosity; no published lists of donations, inspected by public eyes. What was contributed was given unostentatiously, whether a barrel of coffee or the only half bottle of wine in the giver's possession.

About this time one of these large hospitals was to be opened, and the wife of [George W. Randolph,] the then acting secretary of war, offered me the superintendence—rather a startling proposition to a woman used to all the comforts of luxurious life. Foremost among the Virginia women, she had given her resources of mind and means to the sick, and her graphic and earnest representations of the benefit a good and determined woman's rule could effect in such a position settled the result in my mind. The natural idea that such a life would be injurious to the delicacy and refinement of a lady—that her nature would become deteriorated and her sensibilities blunted, was rather appalling. But the first step only costs, and that was soon taken.

A preliminary interview with the surgeon in chief gave necessary confidence. He was energetic—capable—skillful. A man with ready oil to pour upon troubled waters. Difficulties melted away beneath the warmth of his ready interest, and mountains sank into mole-hills when his quick comprehension had surmounted and leveled them. However troublesome daily increasing annoyances became, if they could not be removed, his few and ready words sent applicants and grumblers home satisfied to do the best they could. Wisely he decided to have an educated and efficient woman at the head of his hospital, and having succeeded, never allowed himself to forget that fact.

The day after my decision was made found me at "headquarters," the only two-story building on hospital ground, then occupied by the chief surgeon and his clerks. He had not yet made his appearance that morning, and while awaiting him, many of his corps, who had expected in horror the advent of female supervision, walked in and out, evidently inspecting me. There was at that time a general ignorance on all sides, except among the hospital officials, of the decided objection on the part of the latter to the carrying out of a law which they prognosticated would entail "petticoat government;" but there was no mistaking the stage-whisper which reached my ears from the open door of the office that morning, as the little contract surgeon passed out and informed a friend he met, in a tone of ill-concealed disgust, that *"one of them had come."*

ONE

To those not acquainted with hospital arrangements, some explanations are necessary. To each hospital is assigned a surgeon-in-chief. To each *division* of the hospital, a surgeon in charge. To each *ward* of the division, an assistant surgeon. But when the press of business is great, contract doctors are also put in charge of wards. The surgeon-in-chief makes an inspection each day, calling a board of inferior surgeons to make their report to him. The surgeon in charge is always on the ground, goes through the wards daily, consulting with his assistants and reforming abuses, making his report daily to the surgeon-in-chief. The assistant surgeon has only his one or two wards to attend, passing through them twice each day and prescribing. In cases of danger he calls in the surgeon in charge for advice or assistance. The contract surgeons performed the same duties as assistant surgeons, but ranked below them, as they were not commissioned officers and received less pay. Each ward had its corps of nurses, unfortunately not practised or expert in their duties, as they had been sick or wounded men, convalescing and placed in that position,—however ignorant they might be,—till strong enough for field duty. This arrangement bore very hard upon all interested, and harder upon the sick, as it entailed constant supervision and endless teaching; but the demand for men in the field was too imperative to allow those who were fit for their duties there to be detained for nursing purposes, however skillful they may have become.

Besides these mentioned, the hospital contained an endless horde of stewards and their clerks; surgeons' clerks; commissaries and their clerks; quartermasters and clerks; apothecaries and clerks; baggage-masters; forage-masters; wagon-masters; cooks; bakers; carpenters; shoemakers; ward-inspectors; ambulance-drivers; and many more; forgotten hangers-on, to whom the soldiers gave the name of "hospital rats" in common with would-be invalids who resisted being cured from a disinclination to field service. They were so called, it is to be supposed, from the difficulty of getting rid of either species. Still, many of them were physically unfit for the field.

Among these conflicting elements, all belittled at a time of general enthusiasm by long absence from the ennobling influences of military service, and all striving with rare exceptions to gain the small benefits and few comforts so scarce in the Confederacy, I was introduced that day by the surgeon in charge. He was a cultivated, gentlemanly man, kind-hearted when he remembered to be so, and very much afraid of any responsibility resting upon his shoulders. No preparations had been made by him for his female department. He escorted me into a long, low, whitewashed building, open from end to end, called for two benches, and then, with entire composure, as if surrounding circumstances were most favorable, commenced an aesthetic conversation on *belles lettres,* female influence, and the first, last and only novel published during the war. (It was a translation of *Joseph the Second,* printed on gray and bound in marbled wall-paper.) A neat compliment offered at leave-taking rounded off the interview, with a parting promise from him to send me the carpenter to make partitions and shelves for office, parlor, laundry, pantry and kitchen. The steward was then summoned for consultation, and my representative reign began.

A stove was unearthed; very small, very rusty, and fit only for a family of six. There were then about six hundred men upon the matron's diet list, the illest ones to be supplied with food from my kitchen, and the convalescents from the steward's, called, in contra-distinction from mine, "the big kitchen." Just then my mind could hardly grope through the darkness that clouded it, as to what were my special duties, but one mental spectrum always presented itself—*chicken soup.*

Having vaguely heard of requisitions, I then and there made my first, in very unofficial style. A polite request sent through "Jim" (a small black boy) to the steward for a pair of chickens. They came instantly ready dressed for cooking. Jim picked up some shavings, kindled up the stove, begged, borrowed or stole (either act being lawful to his mind), a large iron pot from the big kitchen. For the first time I cut up with averted eyes a raw bird, and the Rubicon was passed.

My readers must not suppose that this picture applies generally to all our hospitals, or that means and appliances so early in the war for food and comfort, were so meagre. This state of affairs was only the result of accident and some misunderstanding. The surgeon of my hospital naturally thought I had informed myself of the power vested in me by virtue of my position, and, having some experience, would use the rights given me by the law passed in Congress, to arrange my own department; and I, on reading the bill, could only understand that the office was one that dovetailed the duties of housekeeper and cook, nothing more.

In the meantime the soup was boiling, and was undeniably a success, from the perfume it exhaled. Nature may not have intended me for a Florence Nightingale, but a kitchen proved my worth. Frying-pans, griddles, stewpans and coffee-pots soon became my household gods. The niches must have been prepared years previously, invisible to the naked eye but still there.

Gaining courage from familiarity with my position, a venture across the lane brought me to the nearest ward (they were all separate buildings, it must be remembered, covering a half mile of ground in a circle, one story high, with long, low windows opening back in a groove against the inside wall), and, under the first I peeped in, lay the shadow of a man extended on his bed, pale and attennuated.

What woman's heart would not melt and make itself a home where so much needed?

His wants were inquired into, and, like all the humbler class of men, who think that unless they have been living on hog and hominy they are starved, he complained of not having eaten anything "for three mortal weeks."

In the present state of the kitchen larder, there was certainly not much of a choice, and I was as yet ignorant of the capabilities of the steward's department. However, soup was suggested, as a great soother of "misery in his back," and a generous supply of adjectives prefixed for flavor—"nice, hot, good chicken soup." The suggestion was received kindly. If it was very nice he would take some: "he was never, though, much of a hand for drinks." My mind rejected the application of words, but matter not mind, was the subject under consideration.

All my gastronomic experience revolted against soup without the sick man's parsley; and Jim, my acting partner, volunteered to get some at a mysterious place he always called "The Dutchman's," so at last, armed with a bowl full of the decoction, duly salted, peppered, and seasoned, I again sought my first patient.

He rose deliberately—so deliberately that I felt sensible of the great favor he was conferring. He smoothed his tangled locks with a weak hand, took a piece of well-masticated tobacco from between three or four solitary teeth, but still the soup was unappropriated, and it appeared evident that some other preliminaries were to be arranged. The novelty of my position,

added to a lively imagination, suggested fears that he might think it necessary to arise for compliment sake; and hospital clothing being made to suit
the scarcity and expense of homespun, the idea was startling. But my sus-
pense did not continue long; he was only seeking for a brown-covered tract
hid under his pillow.

Did he intend to read grace before meat? No, he simply wanted a pocket-
handkerchief, which cruel war had denied; so without comment a leaf was
quietly abstracted and used for that purpose. The result was satisfactory, for
the next moment the bowl was taken from my hand, and the first spoonful
of soup transmitted to his mouth.

It was an awful minute! My fate seemed to hang upon the fiat of that uneducated palate. A long painful gulp, a "judgmatical" shake of the head, *not* in
the affirmative, and the bowl traveled slowly back to my extended hand.

"My mammy's soup was not like that," he whined. "But I might worry a
little down if it war'n't for them *weeds* a-floating round."

Well! why be depressed? There may not after all be any actual difference
between weeds and herbs.

Two

*A*fter that first day improvements rapidly progressed. Better stoves, and plenty of them, were put up; closets enclosed; china or its substitutes, pottery and tin, supplied. I learned to make requisitions and to use my power. The coffee, tea, milk, and all other luxuries provided for the sick wards, were, through my demand, turned over to me; also a co-laborer with Jim, that young gentleman's disposition proving to be like my old horse, who pulled well and steadily in single harness, but when tried in double team, left all the hard work to the last comer. However, honor to whom honor is due. He gave me many hints which my higher intelligence had overlooked, comprehended by him more through instinct than reason, and was as clever at gathering trophies for my kitchen as Gen. [Benjamin F.] Butler was—for other purposes.

Still my office did not rise above that of chief cook, for I dared not leave my kitchen unattended for a moment, till Dr. [James B.] M[cCaw], one day, passing the window, and seeing me seated on a low bench peeling potatoes, appeared much surprised, and inquired where my cooks were. Explanations followed, a copy of hospital rules was sent for, and authority found to provide the matron's department with suitable attendants. A gentle, sweet-tempered lady, extremely neat and efficient, was appointed assistant matron, also three or four cooks and bakers. Jim and his companion were degraded into drawers of water and hewers of wood; that is to say, these ought to have been their duties, but their occupation became walking gentlemen. On assuming their out-door labors, their allegiance to me ceased, and the trophies which formerly swelled my list of dainties for the sick were nightly carried "down the hill," where everything that was missed disappeared.

Then began the routine of hospital life in regular order. Breakfast at seven in the morning in summer and eight in winter. Coffee, tea, milk, bread of various kinds, and butter or molasses, and whatever meats could be saved from the yesterday's dinner. This was in the first year of the war. Afterwards we were not able to be so luxurious. The quantity supplied would be impartially divided among the wards with the retention of the delicacies for the very ill men.

The ward-masters with their nurses gathered three times a day, for each meal, around my office window adjoining the kitchen, with large wooden trays and piles of plates, waiting to receive the food, each being helped in turn to a fair division. If an invalid craved any particular dish the nurse mentioned the want, and if not contrary to the surgeon's order, it, or its nearest approximation was allowed him.

After breakfast the assistant surgeons visited their respective wards, making out their diet lists, or rather filling them up, for the forms were printed, and only the invalid's name, number of his bed, and his diet—light, half, or full, were required to be specified, also the quantity of whiskey desired for each. Dinner and supper served in the same way, except for the very sick. They had what they desired, in or out of season, and all seemed to object to the nutriment concocted from those tasteless and starchy compounds of wheat, corn and arrowroot, that are so thick and heavy to swallow, and so little nutritious. They were served hot from the fire, or congealed from the ice (for after the suffering caused from the deprivation of ice the first summer of the war was felt, each hospital built its own ice-house, which was well filled by the next season). At two o'clock the regular dinner of poultry, beef, ham, fish and vegetables, was distributed. (After the first year our bill of fare decreased much in variety.) Supper at six. The chief matron sat at her table, the diet lists arranged before her, each day, and managed so that no especial ward should invariably be the first served, although they were named in alphabetical order. Any necessary instructions of the surgeons were noted and attended to, sometimes accompanied with observations of her own, not always complimentary to those gentlemen, nor prudent as regarded herself.

The orders ran somewhat in this fashion: "Chicken soup for twenty—beef tea for forty—tea and toast for fifty." A certain Mr. Jones had expressed his abhorrence of tea and toast, so I asked the nurse why he gave it to him.

He answered that the diet was ordered by the surgeon, but Jones said he would not touch it, for he never ate slops, and so he had eaten nothing for two days.

"Well, what does he wish?"

"The doctor says tea and toast" (reiterating his first remark).

"Did you tell the doctor he would not eat it?"

"*I* told the doctor, and *he* told the doctor."

"Perhaps he did not hear, or understand you."

"Yes, he did. He only said that he wanted that man particularly to have tea and toast, though I told him Jones threw it up regularly; so he put it down again, and said Jones was out of his head, and Jones says the doctor is a fool."

My remark upon this was that Jones could not be so very much out of his head—an observation that entailed subsequent consequences. The habit so common among physicians when dealing with uneducated people, of insisting upon particular kinds of diet, irrespective of the patient's tastes, was a peculiar grievance that no complaint during four years ever remedied.

Although visiting my wards in the morning for the purpose of speaking words of comfort to the sick, and remedying any apparent evils which had been overlooked or forgotten by the surgeons when going their rounds, the fear that the nourishment furnished had not suited the tastes of men debilitated to an extreme not only by disease and wounds, but also by the privations and exposures of camp life, would again take me among them in the afternoon. Then would come heart-sickness and discouragement, for out of a hundred invalids, seventy, on an average, would assert that they had not taken any nourishment whatever. This was partly owing to habit or imitation of others, and partly to the human desire to enlist sympathy. The common soldier has a horror of a hospital, and with the rejection of food comes the hope that weakness will increase proportionally, and a furlough become necessary. Besides, the human palate, to relish good food, must be as well educated as other organs for other purposes. Who appreciates a good painting until his eye is trained, or fine harmony until the ear is cultivated? And why should not the same rule apply to tongue and taste? Men who never before had been sick, or swallowed those starchy, flavorless compounds young surgeons are so fond of prescribing, repudiated them invariably, in spite of my skill in making them palatable. They were suspicious of the *terra incognita* from which they sprang, having had no experience heretofore, and suspicion always engenders disgust.

Daily inspection too, convinced me that great evils still existed under my rule, in spite of my zealous care for my patients. For example, the monthly barrel of whiskey which I was entitled to draw still remained at the dispensary under the guardianship of the apothecary and his clerks, and quarts and pints were issued through any order coming from surgeons or their substitutes, so that the contents were apt to be gone long before I was entitled to draw more, and my sick would suffer for want of the stimulant. There were many suspicious circumstances connected with this *institution;* for the monthly barrel was an institution and a very important one. Indeed, if it is necessary to have a hero for this matter of fact narrative, the whiskey barrel will have to step forward and make his bow.

So again I referred to the hospital bill passed by Congress, which provided that liquors in common with other luxuries, belonged to the matron's department, and in an evil moment, such an impulse as tempted Pandora to open the fatal casket assailed me, and I despatched the bill, flanked by a formal requisition for the liquor. An answer came in the shape of the head surgeon. He declared I would find "the charge most onerous," that "whiskey was required at all hours, sometimes in the middle of the night, and even if I remained at the hospital, he would not like me to be disturbed," "it was constantly needed for medicinal purposes," "he was responsible for its proper application;" but I was not convinced, and withstood all argument and persuasion. He was proverbially sober himself, but I was aware why both commissioned and non-commissioned officers opposed violently the removal of the liquor to my quarters. So, the printed law being at hand for reference, I nailed my colors to the mast, and that evening all the liquor was in my pantry and the key in my pocket.

Three

*T*he first restraints of a woman's presence had now worn away, and the thousand miseries of my position began to make themselves felt. The young surgeons (not all gentlemen, although their profession should have made them aspirants to the character), and the nurses played into each other's hands. If the former were off on a frolic, the latter would conceal the absence of necessary attendance by erasing the date of the diet list of the day before and substituting the proper one, duplicating the prescription also, and thus preventing inquiry. In like manner the assistant surgeons, to whom the nurses were alone responsible, would give them leave of absence, concealing the fact from the head surgeon, which could easily be effected; then the patients would suffer, and complaints from the matron be obnoxious and troublesome, and also entirely out of her line of business. She was to be cook and housekeeper, and nothing more. Added now to other difficulties was the dragonship of the Hesperides, the guarding of the liquefied golden fruit to which access had been open to a certain extent before her reign, and for many, many months the petty persecutions endured from all the small fry around almost exceeded human patience to bear. What the surgeon in charge could do to mitigate the annoyances entailed he conscientiously did; but with the weight of a large hospital on his not very strong mind, and very little authority delegated to him, he could hardly reform abuses or punish silly attacks, so small in the abstract, so great in the aggregate.

The eventful evening when Mr. Jones revolted against tea and toast, my unfortunate remark intended for no particular ear but caught by the nurse, that the patient's intellects could not be confused if he called his surgeon a fool, brought forth a recriminating note to me. It was from that maligned and incensed gentleman, and proved the progenitor of a long series of communications of the same character; a family likeness pervading them all. They generally commenced with "Dr. ——— presents his compliments to the chief matron," continuing with "Mrs.——— and I," and ending with "you and him." They were difficult to understand and more difficult to endure. Accustomed to be treated with extreme deference and courtesy by the highest officials connected with the goverment, moving in the same social grade I had always occupied when beyond hospital bounds, the change was appalling.

The inundation of notes that followed for many months could not have been sent back unopened, the last refuge under the circumstances, for some of them might have related to the well-being of the sick. My pen certainly was ready enough, but could I waste my thunderbolts in such an atmosphere?

The depreciated currency, which purchased only at fabulous prices by this time; the poor pay the government (feeling the necessary of keeping up the credit of its paper) gave to its officials; the natural craving for luxuries that had been but common food before the war, caused appeals to be made to me, sometimes for the applicant, oftener for his sick wife or child, so constantly, that had I given even one-tenth of the gifts demanded there would have been but little left for my patients.

It was hard to refuse, for the plea that it was not mine but merely a charge confided to me, was looked upon as a pretext; outsiders calculating upon the quantity issued to my department and losing sight of the ownership of the quantity received.

Half a dozen convalescent men would lose their tasteless dinner daily at the steward's table, and beg for "anything" which would mean turkey and oysters. Others "had been up all night and craved a cup of coffee and a roll," and as for diseases among commissioned and non-commissioned men, caused by entire destitution of whiskey, and only to be cured by it—their name was legion. Every pound of coffee, every ounce of whiskey, bushel of flour or vegetables duly weighed before delivery, was intended for its particular consumers; who, if they even could not eat or drink what was issued for them watched their property zealously, and claimed it too. So what had I to give away?

The necessity of refusing the live-long day, forced upon naturally generous tempers, makes them captious and uncivil, and under the pressure the soft answer cannot be evoked to turn away wrath. Demands would increase until they amounted to persecutions when the refusals became the rule instead of the exception, and the breach thus made grew wider day by day, until "my hand was against every man, and every man's hand against me."

Besides, there was little gratitude felt in a hospital, and certainly none expressed. The mass of patients were uneducated men, who had lived by the sweat of their brow, and gratitude is an exotic plant, reared in a refined

atmosphere, kept free from coarse contact and nourished by unselfish-
ness. Common natures look only with surprise at great sacrifices and cun-
ningly avail themselves of the benefits they bestow, but give nothing in
return,—not even the satisfaction of allowing the giver to feel that the care
bestowed has been beneficial; *that* might entail compensation of some kind,
and in their ignorance they fear the nature of the equivalent which might
be demanded.

Still, pleasant episodes often occurred to vary disappointments and
lighten duties.

"Kin you writ me a letter?" drawled a whining voice from a bed in one
of the wards, a cold day in '62.

The speaker was an up-country Georgian, one of the kind called "Gou-
bers" by the soldiers generally; lean, yellow, attennuated, with wispy strands
of hair hanging over his high, thin cheek-bones. He put out a hand to detain
me and the nails were like claws.

"Why do you not let the nurse cut your nails?"

"Because I aren't got any spoon, and I use them instead."

"Will you let me have your hair cut then? You can't get well with all that
dirty hair hanging about your eyes and ears."

"No, I can't git my hair cut, kase as how I promised my mammy that I
would let it grow till the war be over. Oh, it's onlucky to cut it!"

"Then I can't write any letter for you. Do what I wish you to do, and
then I will oblige you."

This was plain talking. The hair was cut (I left the nails for another day),
my portfolio brought, and sitting by the side of his bed I waited for further
orders. They came with a formal introduction,—"for Mrs. Marthy Brown."

"My dear Mammy:
"I hope this finds you well, as it leaves me well, and I hope that I shall git a
furlough Christmas, and come and see you, and I hope that you will keep
well, and all the folks be well by that time, as I hopes to be well myself.
This leaves me in good health, as I hope it finds you and—"

But here I paused, as his mind seemed to be going round in a circle, and
asked him a few questions about his home, his position during the last summer's campaign, how he got sick, and where his brigade was at that time.
Thus furnished with some material to work upon, the letter proceeded

rapidly. Four sides were conscientiously filled, for no soldier would think a letter worth sending home that showed any blank paper.

Transcribing his name, the number of his ward and proper address, so that an answer might reach him—the composition was read to him. Gradually his pale face brightened, a sitting posture was assumed with difficulty (for, in spite of his determined effort in his letter "to be well," he was far from convalescence). As I folded and directed it, contributed the expected five-cent stamp, and handed it to him, he gazed cautiously around to be sure there were no listeners.

"Did you writ all that?" he asked, whispering, but with great emphasis.

"Yes."

"Did *I* say all that?"

"I think you did."

A long pause of undoubted admiration—astonishment ensued. What was working in that poor mind? Could it be that Psyche had stirred one of the delicate plumes of her wing and touched that dormant soul?

"Are you married?" the harsh voice dropped very low.

"I am not. At least, I am a widow."

He rose still higher in bed. He pushed away desperately the tangled hay on his brow. A faint color fluttered over the hollow cheek, and stretching out a long piece of bone with a talon attached, he gently touched my arm and with constrained voice whispered mysteriously:

"You wait!"

And readers, I *am* waiting still; and I here caution the male portion of creation who may adore through their mental powers, to respect my confidence, and not seek to shake my constancy.

Other compliments were paid me, perhaps not of so conclusive a nature, and they were noticeable from their originality and novelty, but they were also rare. Expression was not a gift among the common soldiers. "You will wear them little feet away," said a rough Kentuckian, "running around so much. They ar'n't much to boast of anyway." Was not this as complimentary as the lover who compared his mistress's foot to a dream; and much more comprehensible?

At intervals the lower wards, unused except in times of great need, for they were unfurnished with any comforts, would be filled with rough soldiers from camp, sent to recuperate after field service, who may not have seen a female face for months; and though generally too much occupied to notice them, their partly concealed, but determined regard would become embarrassing. One day, while directing arrangements with a ward-master, my attention was attracted by the pertinacious staring of a rough-looking Texan. He walked round and round me in rapidly narrowing circles, examining every detail of my dress, face, and figure; his eye never fixing upon any particular part for a moment but traveling incessantly all over me. It seemed the wonder of the mind at the sight of a new creation. I moved my position; he shifted his to suit the new arrangement—again a change was made, so obviously to get out of his range of vision, that with a delicacy of feeling that the roughest men always treated me with, he desisted from his inspection so far, that though his person made no movement, his neck twisted round to accommodate his eyes, till I supposed some progenitor of his family had been an owl. The men began to titter, and my patience became exhausted.

"What is the matter, my man? Did you never see a woman before?"

"Jerusalem!" he ejaculated, not making the slightest motion towards withdrawing his determined notice, "I never did see such a nice one. Why, you's as pretty as a pair of red shoes with green strings."

These were the two compliments laid upon the shrine of my vanity during four years' contact with thousands of patients, and I commit them to paper to stand as a visionary portrait, to prove to my readers that a woman with attractions similar to a pair of red shoes with green strings must have some claim to the apple of Paris.

Four

Scenes of pathos occurred daily—scenes that wrung the heart and forced the dew of pity from the eyes; but feeling that enervated the mind and relaxed the body was a sentimental luxury that was not to be indulged in. There was too much work to be done, too much active exertion required, to allow the mental or physical powers to succumb. They were severely taxed each day. Perhaps they balanced, and so kept each other from sinking. There was, indeed, but little leisure to sentimentalize, the necessity for action being ever present.

After the battle of Fredericksburg, while giving small doses of brandy to a dying man, a low, pleasant voice, said "Madam." It came from a youth not over eighteen years of age, seeming very ill, but so placid, with that earnest, far-away gaze, so common to the eyes of those who are looking their last on this world. Does God in his mercy give a glimpse of coming peace, past understanding, that we see reflected in the dying eyes into which we look with such strong yearning to fathom what they see? He shook his head in negative to all offers of food or drink or suggestions of softer pillows and lighter covering.

"I want Perry," was his only wish.

On inquiry I found that Perry was the friend and companion who marched by his side in the field and slept next to him in camp, but of whose whereabouts I was ignorant. Armed with a requisition from our surgeon, I sought him among the sick and wounded at all the other hospitals. I found him at Camp Jackson, put him in my ambulance, and on arrival at my own hospital found my patient had dropped asleep. A bed was brought and placed at his side, and Perry, only slightly wounded, laid upon it. Just then the sick boy awoke wearily, turned over, and the half-unconscious eye fixed itself. He must have been dreaming of the meeting, for he still distrusted the reality. Illness had spiritualized the youthful face; the transparent forehead, the delicate brow so clearly defined, belonged more to heaven than earth. As he recognized his comrade the wan and expressionless lips curved into the happiest smile—the angel of death had brought the light of summer skies to that pale face. "Perry," he cried, "Perry," and not another word, but with one last effort he threw himself into his friend's arms, the radiant eyes closed, but the smile still remained—he was dead.

There was but little sensibility exhibited by soldiers for the fate of their comrades in field or hospital. The results of war are here to-day and gone to-morrow. I stood still, spell-bound by that youthful death-bed, when my painful revery was broken upon by a drawling voice from a neighboring bed, which had been calling me by such peculiar names or titles that I had been oblivious to whom they were addressed.

"Look here. I say, Aunty!—Mammy!—You!" Then, in despair, "Missus! Mauma! Kin you gim me sich a thing as a b'iled sweet pur-r-rta-a-a-tu-ur? I b'long to the Twenty-secun' Nor' Ka-a-a-li-i-na rigiment." I told the nurse to remove his bed from proximity to his dead neighbor, thinking that in the low state of his health from fever the sight might affect his nerves, but he treated the suggestion with contempt.

"Don't make no sort of difference to *me;* they dies all around *me* in the field—don't trouble *me*."

The wounded men at this time began to make serious complaints that the liquor issued did not reach them, and no vigilance on my part appeared to check the improper appropriation of it, or lead to any discovery of the thieves in the wards. There were many obstacles to be surmounted before proper precautions could be taken. Lumber was so expensive that closets in each ward were out of the question, and if made locks could not be purchased for any amount of money. The liquor, therefore, when it left my quarters, was open to any passer-by in the wards who would watch his opportunity; so, although I had strong and good reasons for excluding female nurses, the supposition that liquor would be no temptation to them, and would be more apt to reach its proper destination through their care, determined me to engage them.

Unlucky thought, born in an evil hour!

There were no lack of applications when the want was circulated, but my choice hesitated between ladies of education and position, who I knew would be willing to aid me, and the common class of respectable servants. The latter suited best, because it was to be supposed they would be more amenable to authority. They were engaged, and the very sick wards divided among three of them. They were to keep the bed-clothing in order, receive and dispense the liquor, carry any delicacy in the way of food where it was most needed, and in fact do anything reasonable that was requested. The last stipulation was dwelt upon strongly. The next day my new corps were in attendance, and the different liquors, beverages and stimulants delivered to them under the black looks of the ward-masters. No. 1 received hers silently. She was a cross-looking woman from North Carolina, painfully ugly, or rather what is termed hard-featured, and apparently very taciturn; the last quality rather an advantage. She had hardly left my kitchen when she returned with all the drinks, and a very indignant face.

In reply to inquiries made she proved her taciturnity was not chronic. She asserted loudly that she was a decent woman, and "was not going any- where in a place where a man sat up on his bed in his shirt, and the rest laughed—she knew they were laughing at her." The good old proverb that talking is silver but silence is gold had impressed itself on my mind long before this, so I silently took her charge from her, telling her that a hospi- tal was no place for a person of her delicate sensibilities, and at the same time holding up Miss G. and myself (who were young enough to be her daughters), as examples for her imitation.

She answered truly that we acted as we pleased and so would she; and that was the last I saw of her. What her ideas of hospital life were I never inquired, and shall never know.

No. 2 came briskly forward. She was a plausible, light-haired, light-eyed and light-complexioned Englishwoman; very petite, with a high nose. She had come to the hospital with seven trunks, which ought to have been a warning to me, but she brought such strong recommendations from respon- sible parties that they warped my judgment. She received the last trust handed her—an open pitcher of hot punch—with averted head, nose turned aside, and held it at arm's length with a high disdain mounted upon her high nose. Her excuse for this antipathy was that the smell of liquor was "awful," she "could not a-bear it," and "it turned her witals." This was rather suspi- cious, but we deferred judgment.

Dinner was distributed. No. 2 appeared, composed, vigilant and atten- tive to her duties, carrying her delicacies of food to her wards with the assistance of the nurses. No. 3, an inoffensive woman did the same, and all worked well. That afternoon, when I had retired to my little sanctum to take the one hour's rest that I allowed myself each day undisturbed, Miss G. put her head in the door with an apprehensive look and said, "the new matrons wished to see me. "They were admitted, and my high-nosed friend, who had been elected spokeswoman it seems, said after a few preliminaries, with a toss of her head and a couple of sniffs that I "seemed to have made myself very comfortable."

This was assented to graciously. She added that other people were not, who were quite as much entitled to *style*. This also remained undisputed, and then she stated her real grievance, that they "were not satisfied, for I had not invited them to call upon me, or into my room," and "they considered themselves quite as much ladies as I was." I answered I was glad to hear it, and hoped they would always act as ladies should, and in a way suitable to the title. There was an evident desire on her part to say more, but she had not calculated upon the style of reception, and therefore was thrown out beyond her line of action, so she civilly requested me to call and inspect their quarters that they were dissatisfied with. An hour later I did so, and found them sitting around a sociable spittoon, with a friendly box of snuff— dipping! I found it impossible to persuade them that the government was alone responsible for their poor quarters, they persisted in holding me answerable.

The next day, walking through one of the wards under No. 2's charge, I found a part of the building, of about eight to ten feet square, portioned off, a roughly improvised plank partition dividing this temporary room from the rest of the ward. Seated comfortably therein was the new matron, entrenched among her trunks. A neat table and comfortable chair, abstracted from my few kitchen appurtenances, added to her comforts. Choice pieces of crockery, remnants of more luxurious times, that had at one time adorned my shelves, were disposed tastefully around, and the drinks issued by me for the patients were conveniently placed at her elbow. She explained that she kept them there to prevent thefts. Perhaps the nausea communicated from their neighborhood had tinted the high nose higher, and there was a defiant look about her, as if she sniffed the battle afar.

It was very near though, and had to be fought, however disagreeable, so I instantly entered into explanations, short, but polite. Each patient being allowed, by law, a certain number of feet, every inch taken therefrom was so much ventilation lost, and the abstraction of as much space as she had taken for illegal purposes was a serious matter, and conflicted with the rules that governed the hospital. Besides this, no woman was allowed to stay in the wards, for obvious reasons.

No. 2, however, was a sensible person, for she did not waste *her* breath in talking; she merely held her position. An appeal made by me to the surgeon of the ward did not result favorably; he said I had engaged her, she belonged to my corps, and was under my supervision: so I sent for the steward.

The steward of a hospital cannot define exactly what his duties are, the difficulty being to find out what they are not. Whenever it has to be decided who has to fill a disagreeable office, the choice invariably falls upon the steward. So a message was sent to his quarters to request him to compel No. 2 to evacuate her hastily improvised premises. He hesitated long, but engaging at last the services of his assistant, a broad-shouldered fighting character, proceeded to eject the new tenant.

He commenced operations by polite explanations; but they were met in a startling manner. She arose and rolled up her sleeves, advancing upon him as he receded down the ward. The sick and wounded men roared with laughter, cheering her on, and she remained mistress of the field. Dinner preparations served as an interlude and silently suppressed, she as usual made her entrée into the kitchen, received the drinks for her ward and vanished. Half an hour elapsed and then the master of the ward in which she had domiciled herself made his report to me, and recounted a pitiful tale. He was a neat quiet manager, and usually kept his quarters beautifully clean. No. 2, he said, divided the dinner, and whenever she came across a bone in hash or stew, or indeed anything therein displeased her, she took it in her fingers and dashed it upon the floor. With so little to make a hospital gay, this peculiar episode was a god-send to the soldiers, and indeed to all the lookers on. The surgeons stood laughing, in groups, the men crowded to the windows of the belligerent power, and a *coup-d'état* became necessary.

"Send me the carpenter!" I felt the spirit of Boadicea. The man stepped up; he had always been quiet, civil and obedient.

"Come with me into Ward E."

A few steps took us there.

"Knock down that partition and carry away those boards." It was *un fait accompli*.

But the victory was not gained, only the fortifications stormed and taken, for almost hidden by flying splinters and dust, No. 2 sat among her seven trunks enthroned like Rome upon her seven hills.

The story furnishes no further interest, but the result was very annoying. She was put into my ambulance very drunk by this time and sent away, her trunks sent after her. The next day, neatly dressed, she managed to get an interview with the medical director, enlisted his sympathy by a plausible appeal and description of her desolate condition. "A refugee," or "refewgee," as she called herself, "trying to make her living decently," and receiving an order to report at our hospital, was back there by noon. Explanations had to be written, and our surgeon-in-chief to interfere with his authority, before we could get rid of her.

FIVE

*A*bout this time (April, 1863), an attack on Drewry's Bluff, which guarded Richmond on the James river side, was expected, and it was made before the hospital was in readiness to receive the wounded. The cannonading could be heard distinctly in the city, and dense smoke descried rising from the battle-field. The Richmond people had been too often, if not through the wars at least within sight and hearing of its terrors, to feel any great alarm.

The inhabitants lying in groups, crowded the eastern brow of the hill above Rocketts and the James river; overlooking the scene, and discussing the probable results of the struggle; while the change from the dull, full boom of the cannon to the sharp rattle of musketry could be easily distinguished. The sun was setting amidst stormy, purple clouds; and when low upon the horizon sent long slanting rays of yellow light from beneath them, athwart the battle scene, throwing it in strong relief. The shells burst in the air above the fortifications at intervals, and with the aid of glasses dark blue masses of uniforms could be distinguished, though how near the scene of action could not be discerned. About eight o'clock the slightly wounded began to straggle in with a bleeding hand, or contused arm or head, bound up in any convenient rag.

Their accounts were meagre, for men in the ranks never know anything about general results—they almost always have the same answer ready, "We druv 'em nowhere."

In another half-hour, vehicles of all kinds crowded in, from a wheelbarrow to a stretcher, and yet no orders had been sent me to prepare for the wounded. Few surgeons had remained in the hospital; the proximity to the field tempting them to join the ambulance committee, or ride to the scene of action; and the officer of the day, left in charge, naturally objected to my receiving a large body of suffering men with no arrangements made for their comfort, and but few in attendance. I was preparing to leave for my home at the Secretary of the Navy, where I returned every night, when the pitiful sight of the wounded in ambulances, furniture wagons, carts, carriages, and every kind of vehicle that could be impressed detained me. To keep them unattended to, while being driven from one full hospital to another, entailed unnecessary suffering, and the agonized outcry of a desperately wounded man to "take him in, for God's sake, or kill him," decided me to countermand the order of the surgeon in charge that "they must be taken elsewhere, as we had no accommodations prepared." I sent for him, however. He was a kind-hearted, indolent man, but efficient in his profession, and a gentleman; and seeing my extreme agitation, tried to reason with me, saying our wards were full, except a few vacant and unused ones, which our requisitions had failed to furnish with proper bedding and blankets. Besides, a large number of the surgeons were absent, and the few left would not be able to attend to all the wounds at that late hour of the night. I proposed in reply that the convalescent men should be placed on the floor on blankets, or bed-sacks filled with straw, and the wounded take their place, and, purposely construing his silence into consent, gave the necessary orders, eagerly offering my services to dress simple wounds, and extolling the strength of my nerves. He let me have my way (may *his* ways be of pleasantness and his paths of peace), and so, giving Miss G. orders to make an unlimited supply of coffee, tea, and stimulants, armed with lint, bandages, castile soap, and a basin of warm water, I made my first essays in the surgical line. I had been spectator often enough to be skillful. The first object that needed my care was an Irishman. He was seated upon a bed with his hands crossed, wounded in both arms by the same bullet. The blood was soon washed away, wet lint applied, and no bones being broken, the bandages easily arranged.

"I hope that I have not hurt you much," I said with some trepidation.

"These are the first wounds that I ever dressed."

"Sure they be the most illegant pair of hands that ever touched me, and the lightest," he gallantly answered. "And I am all right now."

From bed to bed till long past midnight, the work continued. Fractured limbs were bathed, washed free from blood and left to the surgeon to set. The men were so exhausted by forced marches, lying in entrenchments and loss of sleep that few even awoke during the operations. If aroused to take nourishment or stimulant they received it with closed eyes, and a speedy relapse into unconsciousness. The next morning, but few had any recollection of the events of the night previous.

There were not as many desperate wounds among the soldiers brought in that night as usual. Strange to say, the ghastliness of wounds varied much in the different battles, perhaps from the nearness or distance of contending parties. One man was an exception and enlisted my warmest sympathy. He was a Marylander although serving in a Virginia company. There was such strength of resignation in his calm blue eye.

"Can you give me a moment?" he said.

"What shall I do for you?"

"Give me some drink to revive me, that I do not die before the surgeon can attend to me."

His pulse was strong but irregular, and telling him that a stimulant might induce fever, and ought only to be administered with a doctor's prescription, I inquired where was he wounded.

Right through the body. Alas!

The doctor's dictum was, "No hope: give him anything he asks for;" but five days and nights I struggled against this decree, fed my patient with my own hands, using freely from the small store of brandy in my pantry and cheering him by words and smiles. The sixth morning on my entrance he tamed an anxious eye on my face, the hope had died out of his, for the cold sweat stood in beads there, useless to dry, so constantly were they renewed. What comfort could I give? Only silently open the Bible, and read to him without comment the ever-living promises of his Maker. Glimpses too of that abode where the "weary are at rest." Tears stole down his cheek, but he was not comforted.

"I am an only son," he said, "and my mother is a widow. Go to her, if you ever get to Baltimore, and tell her that I died in what I consider the defense of civil rights and liberties. I may be wrong. God alone knows. Say how kindly I was nursed, and that I had all I needed. I cannot thank you, for I have no breath, but we will meet up there." He pointed upward and closed his eyes, that never opened again upon this world.

Six

$\mathcal{E}$arlier than this, while hospitals were still partly unorganized, soldiers were brought in from camp or field, and placed in divisions of them, irrespective of rank or state; but soon the officers had more comfortable quarters provided apart from the privates, and separate divisions were also appropriated to men from different sections of the country.

There were so many good reasons for this change that explanations are hardly necessary. Chief among them, was the ease through which, under this arrangement, a man could be found quickly by reference to the books of each particular division. Schedules of where the patients of each State were quartered were published in the daily papers, and besides the materials furnished by government, States and associations, were thus enabled to send satisfactory food and clothing for private distribution. Thus immense contributions, coming weekly from these sources, gave great aid, and enabled us to have a reserved store when government supplies failed.

To those cognizant of these facts, it appeared as if the non-fighting people of the Confederacy had worked as hard and exercised as much self-denial as the soldiers in the field. There was an indescribable pathos lurking at times at the bottom of these heterogeneous home boxes, put up by anxious wives, mothers and sisters; a sad and mute history shadowed forth by the sight of rude, coarse homespun pillow-cases or pocket handkerchiefs, adorned even amid the turmoil of war and poverty of means with an attempt at a little embroidery, or a simple fabrication of lace for trimming. The silent tears dropped over these tokens will never be sung in song or told in story. The little loving expedients to conceal the want of means which each woman resorted to, thinking that if her loved one failed to benefit by the result, other mothers might reap the advantage, is a history in itself.

Piles of sheets, the cotton carded and spun in the one room at home where the family perhaps lived, ate, and slept in the backwoods of Georgia; bales of blankets called so by courtesy, but only the drawing-room carpets, the pride of the heart of thrifty housewives, perhaps their only extravagance in better days, but now cut up for field use. Dozens of pillow slips, not of the coarse product of the home loom, which would be too harsh for the cheek of the invalid, but of the fine bleached cotton of better days, suggesting personal clothing sacrificed to the sick. Boxes of woolen shirts, like Joseph's many-colored coat, created from almost every dressing-gown or flannel skirt in the country.

A thousand evidences of the loving care and energetic labor of the poor, patient ones at home, telling an affecting story that knocked hard at the gates of the heart, were the portals ever so firmly closed; and with all these came letters written by poor ignorant ones who often had no knowledge of how such communications should be addressed.

These letters, making inquiries concerning patients from anxious relatives at home, directed oftener to my office than my name, came in numbers, and were queer mixtures of ignorance, bad grammar, worse spelling and simple feeling. However absurd the style, the love that filled them chastened and purified them. Many are stored away, and though irresistibly ludicrous, are too sacred to print for public amusement.

In them could be detected the prejudices of the different sections. One old lady in upper Georgia wrote a pathetic appeal for a furlough for her son. She called me "My dear sir," while still retaining my feminine address, and though expressing the strongest desire for her son's restoration to health, entreated in moving accents that if his life could not be saved, that he should not be buried in "Ole Virginny *dirt,*"—rather a derogatory term to apply to the sacred soil that gave birth to the presidents—the soil of the Old Dominion.

Almost all of these letters told the same sad tale of destitution of food and clothing, even shoes of the roughest kind being either too expensive for the mass or unattainable by the expenditure of any sum, in many parts of the country. For the first two years of the war, privations were lightly dwelt upon and courageously borne, but when want and suffering pressed heavily as times grew more stringent, there was a natural longing for the stronger heart and frame to bear part of the burden. Desertion is a crime that meets generally with as much contempt as cowardice, and yet how hard for the husband or father to remain inactive in winter quarters, knowing that his wife and little ones were literally starving at home—not even *at home,* for few homes were left.

Our hospital had till now (the summer of 1863), been appropriated to the Gulf States, when an order was issued to transfer and make it entirely Virginian. The cause of this change was unknown, but highly agreeable, for the latter were the very best class of men in the field; intelligent, manly, and reasonable, with more civilized tastes and some desire to conform to rules that were conducive to their health. Besides this, they were a hardier race, and were more inclined to live than die,—a very important taste in a hospital,—so that when the summer campaigns were over, the wards would be comparatively empty. The health of the army improved wonderfully after the first year's exposure had taught them to take proper precautions, and they had become accustomed to the roughnesses of field life. Time was given me, by this lightening of heretofore strenuous duties, to seek around and investigate the mysteries of the arrangements of other hospitals beside my own, and see how my neighbors managed their responsibilities. While on the search for material for improvement, I found a small body of Marylanders, who, having had no distinct refuge awarded them, were sent wherever circumstances made it convenient to lodge them.

There had been, from the breaking out of the war, much petty criticism, privately and publicly expressed, concerning the conduct and position of the Marylanders who had thrown their fortunes in the Confederate scale, and a great deal of ill-feeling engendered. Sister States have never been amicable, but it was not until my vocation drew my attention to the fact that I became aware of the antagonism existing. The Virginians complained that the Marylanders had come south to install themselves in the comfortable clerkships, and to take possession of the lazy places, while those filling them defended their position on the ground that efficient men were required in the departments, as well as the field, and that their superior capacity as clerks was recognized and rewarded without any desire, on their part, to shun field duty. They were unfortunate, as they labored under the disadvantage of harboring, as reputed fellow citizens, every gambler, speculator or vagabond, who, anxious to escape military duty, managed to procure, in some way, exemption papers proving him a native of their so-considered neutral State. An adverse feeling towards them, report said, extended even to the hospitals through which they were scattered, and I endeavored long, but unsuccessfully, to induce Dr. Moore (the Confederate surgeon-general), to inaugurate some building for their use. He was averse to any arrangement of this kind, not from prejudice, but a conviction of the expense and trouble of small establishments of this nature.

Not succeeding I made a personal application to the surgeon-in-chief of my own establishment, to allow me to appropriate a certain number of my own wards to them, and with the ready courtesy he always accorded me, he immediately gave consent.

In the decided objections of surgeons generally to taking charge of Marylanders there was an element more amusing than offensive, and the dismay of the head of our hospital when he heard of my arrangements was ludicrous in the extreme, and our opinions hardly reconcilable from our different standpoints. To a woman there was a touch of romance in the self-denial exercised, the bravery displayed and the hardships endured by a body of men, who were fighting for what was to them an abstract question, as far as they were concerned. No one with any reasoning powers could suppose that Maryland in event of success could ever become a sister State of the Confederacy. Then the majority of them were very young men, who, well born, well nurtured and wealthy, accustomed too to all the luxuries of life, served then, and even to the end as privates, when less deserving men who had commenced their career in the ranks had made interest and risen, as much through political favor as personal bravery. Luxuries received from other States for their soldiers, which though trifling in themselves were so gratifying to their recipients could not come to them; the furlough, that El Dorado to the sick soldier, was the gold which could not be grasped, for there was no home that could be reached. Even letters, those electric conductors from heart to heart, came sparingly after long detention, often telling of the loss of the beloved at home, months after the grave had closed upon them.

In antagonism to these ideas were the strong objections of our head surgeon to this arrangement of mine, and they too were reasonable. The fact of there being an unusual amount of intelligence and independence among these men made them more difficult to manage, as they were less submissive to orders. They were aware of how much they were entitled to, in food, surgical and medical attendance and general comfort; and were not afraid to speak loudly and openly of neglect towards them or of incapacity in their rulers, so that whether ragged, helpless or sick they bore a striking resemblance to Hans Andersen's leather soldier. That historical personage, though lame in the leg, minus an arm and eye, with a mashed head, all the gilt rubbed off of his back and lying in a gutter, held his own opinion and gave it on all occasions. The result of this was that there existed a pretty general objection to them as patients, as they were, to say the least, awkward

customers. I might whisper an aside very low and confidential of sick men
who should have followed the good old wholesome rule of "early to bed
and early to rise" taking their physic obediently in the morning, but disappearing at night,—"dew in the morning and mist at night,"—and I might
also tell of passes altered and furloughs lengthened when there was no
fighting going on, all very wicked, but certainly nothing unmanly or dis-
honorable. They never lingered around when honor called, and their record
needs no additional tribute from my humble pen. When sectional feelings
shall have died away and a fair narration of the Confederate struggle be written, they will find their laurel leaves fresh and green.

But to return to domestic details. My new wards were prepared, freshly
whitewashed, and adorned with cedar boughs for the reception of the old
line Maryland cavalry, and during their sojourn I experienced to its fullest
extent the pleasure of ministering to the wants of grateful and satisfied soldiers. They brightened a short interval of laborious and harassing labors
that lasted over four years, and left a sunny spot for memory to dwell on.
After their departure many more of their State came, generally infantry,
and difficulties still continued. It was impossible to give them their due
share of attention, so great was the feeling of jealousy existing. If an invalid
required special attention, and he proved to be a Marylander, though perhaps ignorant myself of the fact, many eyes watched me, and complaints
were made to the nurses, and from them to the surgeons, till a report of
partiality to them on my part made to the surgeon-in-chief, called forth a
remonstrance on his part, and a request that all patients should be treated
alike. Then came an unpleasant season of bickering and dissatisfaction, so
that fearing I might be to blame in part, I studiously at last avoided inquir-
ing to what corps a man belonged.

A courier of General A. P. Hill's, very badly wounded, had been invalided
for some time, and desirous of offering him some inducement to bear his
fate more patiently, I had invited him to dine in my office, as soon as he
could use his crutches. An invitation of this kind was often extended to men
similarly situated; not that there were delicacies retained in my kitchen that
did not reach the wards, but the request was a courtesy, and the food would
be hot from the fire, and more comfortably served. Unfortunately he was
a Marylander, and that some adverse report had been made was proved by
an order attached to my window during the day, explaining that no patient

would be permitted to enter the matron's department under any circumstances, on penalty of punishment. This was uncalled-for and galling, so I pulled it down first, and then carried my complaint to the surgeon-in-chief. No one ever applied to him in vain for either justice or courtesy. He naturally was unwilling to countermand this order positively, but told me significantly that although the hospital was to a certain extent under the control of the surgeon in charge, and subject to his orders, the private rooms, as well as kitchen and laundry attached to the matron's department were under my management. As a woman will naturally sacrifice her comfort, convenience, pleasure, and privacy to have her own way, the result must be evident. My sleeping-room became a dining-room, and for the future I made what use of it I pleased, returning every night to my quarters at the Secretary's. The next annoyance was the disappearance of all the Maryland patients; their wards being found empty one morning, and "no man living could tell where they had gone." However, when the flesh-pots of the forsaken land were steaming at dinner-time, a small group revealed themselves of the missing tribes, and clustered around my window with cup and plate. They belonged to the infantry, and seemed unable to bear their exile. This continued for a couple of days, the applicants increasing at each meal, till a second visit to Dr. M[cCaw] with a representation of the impossibility of feeding men for whom no rations had been drawn brought about a rescinding of the order for their exile, and from that time they and all of their corps who came to me were unmolested.

SEVEN

*F*eminine sympathy being much more demonstrative than masculine, particularly when compared with a surgeon's unresponsiveness, who inured to the aspects of suffering, has more control over his professional feelings, the nurses often summoned me when only the surgeon was needed. One very cold night the same year, 1863, when sleeping at my hospital rooms, an answer was made to my demand as to who was knocking and what was wanted. The nurse from the nearest ward said, something was wrong with Fisher.

Instructing him to find the doctor immediately and hastily getting on some clothing I hurried to the scene, for Fisher was an especial favorite. He was quite a young man, of about twenty years of age, who had been wounded ten months previously very severely, high up on the leg near the hip, and who by dint of hard nursing, good food and plenty of stimulant had been given a fair chance for recovery. The bones of the broken leg had slipped together, then lapped, and nature anxious as she always is to help herself had thrown a ligature across, uniting the severed parts; but after some time the side curved out, and the wounded leg was many inches shorter than its fellow. He had been the object of sedulous care on the part of all—surgeons, ward-master, nurse and matron, and the last effort made to assist him was by the construction of an open cylinder of pasteboard, made in my kitchen, of many sheets of coarse brown paper, cemented together with very stiff paste, and baked around the stove-pipe. This was to clasp by its own prepared curve the deformed hip, and be a support for it when he was able to use his crutches.

He had remained through all his trials, stout, fresh and hearty, interesting in appearance, and so gentle-mannered and uncomplaining that we all loved him. Supported on his crutches he had walked up and down his ward for the first time since he was wounded, and seemed almost restored. That same night he turned over and uttered an exclamation of pain.

Following the nurse to his bed, and turning down the covering, a small jet of blood spurted up. The sharp edge of the splintered bone must have severed an artery. I instantly put my finger on the little orifice and awaited the surgeon. He soon came—took a long look and shook his head. The explanation was easy; the artery was imbedded in the fleshy part of the thigh and could not be taken up. No earthly power could save him.

There was no object in detaining Dr. ———. He required his time and his strength, and long I sat by the boy, unconscious himself that any serious trouble was apprehended. The hardest trial of my duty was laid upon me; the necessity of telling a man in the prime of life, and fullness of strength that there was no hope for him.

It was done at last, and the verdict received patiently and courageously, some directions given by which his mother would be informed of his death, and then he turned his questioning eyes upon my face.

"How long can I live?"

"Only as long as I keep my finger upon this artery." A pause ensued. God alone knew what thoughts hurried through that heart and brain, called so unexpectedly from all earthly hopes and ties. He broke the silence at last.

"You can let go—"

But I could not. Not if my own life had trembled in the balance. Hot tears rushed to my eyes, a surging sound to my ears, and a deathly coldness to my lips. The pang of obeying him was spared me, and for the first and last time during the trials that surrounded me for four years, I fainted away. No words can do justice to the uncomplaining nature of the Southern soldier. Whether it arose from resignation or merely passive submission, yet when shown in the aggregate in a hospital, it was sublime. Day after day, whether lying wasted by disease or burning up with fever, torn with wounds or sinking from debility, a groan was seldom heard. The wounded wards would be noisily gay with singing, laughing, fighting battles o'er and o'er again, and playfully chaffing each other by decrying the troops from different States, each man applauding his own. When listening to them one would suppose that the whole Southern army with the exception of a few companies from the speaker's section of the country, were cowards. The up-country soldiers, born in the same States as those they derided, went even further and decried "them fellows from the seaboard, who let us do all the fighting." The Georgians would romance of how the South Carolinians laid down at such a battle, refusing to charge, and how they had to "charge right over them." The Mississippians of the backwardness of the Tennessee troops, who "would never go into action unless led by their commanding general." The Virginians told bitter stories of the rowdy-ism of the Maryland volunteers, who were "always spreeing it in the city, and dancing attendance on the women," and the North Carolinians caught it on all sides, though their record is undoubtedly a most gallant one. Taken in the mass, the last were certainly most forlorn specimens, and their drawl was insufferable. Besides, they never under any circumstances would give me the satisfaction of hearing that they relished or even ate any food that was issued from my kitchen. "Say, can I have some sweet soup?" whined a voice from one bed, and "Look here, can I have some sour soup?" came from another. The sweet soup upon explanation proved to be stirred custard; the sour a mystery until the receipt was given. "You jist put a crock of buttermilk on the fire, and let it come to a bile; then mix up the yaller of an egg with some corn flour to make a paste; then punch off pieces of the dough, and bile them with the soup; with lots of pepper and salt." The buttermilk when so tested by heat resolved itself into a sea of whey with a hard ball of curds in the center. I carried the saucepan to his bedside to show the results of his culinary directions; but he merely shook his head and remarked carelessly that "his mammy's soup did not look like that."

Many would not eat unless furnished with food to which they had been accustomed at home, and as unreasoning as brutes resisted nutriment and thus became weaker day after day; and whatever was new to the eye or palate was received suspiciously. Liquids in the form of soups, tea or coffee they turned from with disgust, so that the ordinary diet of invalids was inefficient in their case. Buttermilk seemed especially created by nature for wounded patients; they craved it with a drunkard's thirst, and great, strong men have turned away from all else and implored a drink of sweet milk. We had a very short supply of this towards the end of the war, and I remember a stalwart Kentuckian, one of Morgan's men, insisting upon the rare luxury of one cup-full. He had been for many months on a raid far out of Confederate limits, and returning slightly wounded, had no idea of the scarcity of forage that made our cows so dry. His pleading became really affecting, till at last rallying, I told him: "Why man! the very babies of the Confederacy have given up drinking milk, and here are you, six feet two, crying for it." Little poetical effusions were often thrust under my cabin door, and also notes of all kinds from my patients. Among them one day was a well-written and worded request from a young man who had been indisposed with that most hateful of all annoyances to soldiers—the itch; that shirt of Nessus, which when once attached to the person clings there pertinaciously. It begged me when at leisure to give him an interview, telling me his ward, name, and bed. He proved to be educated, and a gentleman from the upper part of Alabama, which had been colonized by the best class of South Carolinians; and he wished to enlist any influence I might possess in his favor, to endeavor to get him a furlough.

His story was interesting. Engaged to a young girl, the preparations made, the ring even bought (he wore it next his heart), and the marriage day fixed, they heard the first rumors of war, and patriotism urging him to enlist, the parents of his sweetheart naturally refused to allow him to consummate the engagement until peace was restored. The desire to see her again became almost unbearable, and feeling sincere sympathy with him, and the hardship of the case, I tried but in vain to have him furloughed. The campaign of 1864 had opened and every man was needed in the field.

The finale of my story is a sad one, as are almost all stories in time of war. He was killed while repelling with his brigade the attack on Petersburg, and the little history confided to me resolved itself into a romance one night, that found shape and form:

> "ICH HABE GELEBT UND GELIEBT."
> The bride's robe is ready, the bridesmaids are bid,
> The groom clasps the circlet, so cautiously hid;
> For a home is now waiting a mistress to claim
> A lover, a wife, for his house, heart and name.
> There is peace in the homestead and mirth in the hall—
> The steed idly stands at his rack in the stall,
> The whole land is teeming with prosperous life,
> For lost are all memories of carnage and strife.
> With rich golden harvest the ripe hills are blest,
> And God's providence stands revealed and confessed.
>
> ~
>
> No priest blessed that union, no ring wed that hand;
> With anger and discord soon rang the whole land;
> Through all its wide domains the dread tidings rang
> Of bloodshed. The lover was first in the van.

"My own one! I leave thee, those dear arms unfold.
Wouldst wed with the timid—the doubtful—the cold?
No union could bless till our country be free,
So onward for liberty, glory—and thee!"

~

Right bravely fought he till sunlight lying low
Discovered a field that had left him no foe;
But when in the flush of a victory gained,
Deep in dreams of his love—his honor unstained,
He wended his way to the home of his heart
From her side ne'er to swerve, from her love ne'er to part,
Hast'ning on with his tidings he knew she would prize—
His heart on his lips and his soul in his eyes;
Laid low by a shot courage could not repel
At the feet of a mightier victor—he fell!
And the bride that he left? What needs it to say
Her doom was a woman's,—to watch, wait and pray.
The heat of the struggle nerves man for the strife,
But bitter at home is her battle of life,
When far from the conflict, unheeded, alone,
Her brain in a flame, but her heart like a stone,
She patiently waits to hear one life is won,
Or silently prays to say—His will be done!

Eight

The whiskey barrel, as I have said before, and suppose I shall often say again, had been a bone of contention from the beginning, and as it afterward proved, continued so to the end. Liquor commanded an enormous price in Dixie, and often if its lovers had the means to procure it, the opportunity was wanting, as the hospital was some distance from Richmond. When first installed in my office, the desire to conciliate, and the belief that men generally had some conscience even on the whiskey question led me to yield to urgent solicitations for it from many quarters; but the demands increased fearfully upon any concession. A reference to Dr. M[cCaw] about this matter settled the heretofore open question. The doctor said the liquor was intended exclusively for the use of patients, and should only be used through a prescription accompanied by a written order. Also that I was personally responsible for the quantity confided to my care, and must each month produce the surgeon's receipts to balance with the number of gallons drawn from the medical purveyor. There were at different times half a dozen surgeons and officials around, who absolutely made my life wretched by their importunities, and yet who could not be sent away except by preferring charges against them, and proving those charges; for my hospital was a military organization. I did not feel inclined to brave the publicity of preferred charges, for I seemed to have no recognized rank, and if even I could prove them, the complaints made would be ludicrously petty in detail, though distracting as mosquito bites in the aggregate.

The modes adopted to outflank me were named "legion." Some of them can be recalled. A quart bottle of whiskey would be ordered by the officer of the day for each ward, for night use, so that it would be ready at hand should any of the patients need this stimulant during the night. The next morning, on inquiry being made, there had been no case requiring its use, but the bottles would be empty, and expostulation on my part be met with explanations that the rats (who were a very plague), had knocked all the bottles over. On refusing to honor any more demands of the same kind, not believing in the rat story, the surgeon in charge would be appealed to, hear all sides, and favor none. This was just what I anticipated and wanted, for having, for the first few months of my occupation, lived in a state of active terror for fear of violating rules, however injurious the results of obeying, I recompensed myself from that time till the end of my sojourn by acting exactly as I thought right, braving the consequences and preferring to be attacked to attacking. One mode of annoying me was particularly offensive— sending a negro boy with a cup and a simple request for whiskey, as if it was the most natural act in the world. At first a polite refusal would be written, but if this mode should have been persevered in, a private secretary would have been necessary; so in time it was replaced by a curt "No." A few minutes later the boy would again stand before me with the same message, and this would occur half a dozen times consecutively. I did not believe in vicarious punishment, so could not make the messenger responsible—he was compelled to obey; and sometimes, stung to irritation by this senseless pertinacity, I would write a note to the offending party, brief but sharp. The reply would be the same silly question I so often had to meet: "Did Mrs. —— consider herself a lady when she wrote such notes?" "No," was always the indignant answer. "How could she be, when brought into contact with such elements?" It was strange, with so little outward self-assertion, always dressed in Georgia homespun, often the worse for wear, leather shoes, worsted gloves, and half the time with a skillet or coffee-pot in my hands, that all the common element around me should contest my right to a title to which I never aspired in words.

This fact, which must have been patent to them from the active persecution it entailed, seemed to be a crying grievance. My life at my hospital quarters when relieved from care for the patients was exclusive, from habit, inclination and prudence. Living a great part of my time away from all intercourse with my own sex, in a solitude that was unbroken after dark, it was better that no intimacies should be formed and no preferences shown; and in an exposed position where Argus eyes were always watching, a woman could not be too careful.

But still the wars of the whiskey barrel continued. One day the men of one of the distant wards sent for me in the absence of their ward-master, and complained that the liquor issued for them never reached them. All concurred in this report, and said the champagne bottles in which it was kept were hid behind a certain vacant bed, from whence they would be abstracted that night. A search on my part brought them to light, still full, although the hour of administering had long past. The ward-master was summoned, the full bottles exhibited, and expressing my surprise at the inhumanity and dishonesty of one I had heretofore thought so honest, I warned him of the consequences that would result to him. His protestations were so earnest that he never tasted liquor, that I could not disbelieve him. What then had "become of the quantity issued, had he sold it?"

The charge was met by indignant surprise, and then the truth began to dawn upon me. That he had been false to his charge and his patients was true, if even he had not been guilty of taking it, and I warned him that on my representing the matter to the proper authorities he would be sent to the field. An hour after this conversation the surgeon of his ward entered my office with belligerent aspect.

"Did you assert, Madam, that you intended sending my ward-master to the field?"

"I said I intended laying the facts concerning the disappearance of the liquor before the proper authorities."

"I consider myself responsible, Madam, for the liquor used in my wards."

"If you do, you fail to be sure that it reaches its destination, so I intend in future to see that it does."

"If you mean that my ward-master drinks it, you are mistaken; he does not take any stimulant."

"I know he does not," I answered quietly, "and I also know who does." He changed color, and passing him I walked into my little sanctum adjoining the office. To my astonishment he kicked back the door and also entered.

"Doctor, this is my private room," I said, "to which no one is admitted. Be kind enough to leave."

"Not until you explain," he answered, throwing himself at full length upon the couch.

This was just far enough for him to venture. I threw back my window, and called to the sentry to order up a sergeant and file of the guard. In a few minutes the ring of their muskets outside sounded, and taking out my watch, I placed it on the table by him.

"I will give you five minutes," I said, "to leave my room. If you are not gone by that time, commissioned officer as you are, and gentleman as you ought to be, I will have you taken to the guard-house, and then explain this matter to the surgeon-general."

He waited a minute or two, soliloquizing audibly that I must fancy myself the Secretary of War, and he would make me know my position, but soon made up his mind that discretion was the better part of valor, and left. Proper measures were no doubt taken to punish such conduct, for though I made no complaint, there were no secrets in a hospital, and after a few weeks he disappeared, sent no doubt to that Botany Bay—"the front." He took a gallant leave of his associates, hinting that his talents demanded a wider field of action than a hospital.

But the tables were about to be turned. Not forever would I be allowed to carry war into the enemy's country, or be the sole defender of that friend by whom I had stood so gallantly. The whiskey barrel was destined after all to be turned into a weapon of offense.

The bold man who thus declared hostilities, and by a *coup-de-guerre* changed the whole nature of the war from offensive to defensive tactics, had been bar-keeper in a Georgia tavern, afterwards a clerk in a Macon dispensary, in order to escape field duty. Coming to Richmond he passed the board of surgeons by a process known only to themselves, which often rejected good practitioners, and gave appointments to apothecary boys.

Fate sent him to our hospital, where the brilliant idea struck him to check thefts of whiskey in the feminine department. He inaugurated his plans by ordering a pint of it for a single patient.

The etiquette of a hospital enjoins that no one but the chief surgeon shall dispute an inferior surgeon's prescription, so I carried this generous order to the chief, received his instructions not to exceed the usual "from two to four ounces" without being served with a formal requisition signed by the surgeon in charge, and so I wrote this gentleman (a contract surgeon) a few lines, courteously explanatory of my reasons for so cutting him down. This matter being arranged, I forgot all about it, but the next day the blow was struck; the following note being handed to me:

"HOSPITAL, Richmond, April 3, 1864.

"The Chief Matron:—Is respectfully asked to state the amount of water used as compared with amount of whiskey in making toddy. Also if strength of toddy has been uniform since January 1st, 1863. Also if any change has taken place in diluting within the same period. She will also state what the change has been; also when made, and by whose authority.

Respectfully,

"——————— ————,

"Assistant Surgeon in charge."

These questions, if even he had any right to ask them (which he had not), were simply absurd. With hundreds of men requiring different drinks many times each day, ordered by numerous surgeons, prepared to suit different stages of disease and palate, no hour bringing the same orders, how could any kind of a correct statement be made, even if I was willing to make it? But there was a great deal of amusement in the idea of letting him suppose he had alarmed me. Perhaps, as the day was very wet, and the wards rather empty, we might enact a small comedy; so I sat down and answered in full, respectfully, feeling very charitably that he was welcome to all the information he could extract from the five closely-written sheets of foolscrap I despatched him.

In this document, polite, officially formal and as officially obscure, I thought I had succeeded in showing my correspondent that his questions could not be answered satisfactorily, but that I was much alarmed at his asking them. That I did not succeed in regard to his first inquiry was proved by the following, which came after an hour's delay.

"HOSPITAL, April 3rd, 1864.

"Chief Matron:——Is respectfully called upon to state what amount of whiskey has been given to each patient when amount has not been stated or expressed by surgeon, or assistant surgeon, upon the rolls, but instead 'whiskey three times a day,' and shown upon the rolls which I send you.

"Respectfully,
"——————— ————,

"Assistant Surgeon in charge."

No solemn pages greeted him in answer this time. My rejoinder was concise and to the point.

"HOSPITAL, April 3rd, 1864.

"The Chief Matron regrets that she is too busily engaged to give any more voluminous explanations, being at this moment up to her elbows in ginger-bread."

Then the sleeping lion was roused, for almost instantly the reply was brought me, and an alarming finale it was.

"HOSPITAL, April 3rd, 1864.

"Chief Matron: Is hereby informed that if she willfully and contumaciously refuses to give me such information as I demand, and she is possessed of, thereby obstructing the duty I feel myself called upon to perform, she must be prepared to *meet* the responsibility upon *your own shoulders.*

"Respectfully,

"_____ _____,

"Assistant Surgeon in charge."

A serious but sharp rejoinder sent to this gentleman, trying to show him that he had no authority to propound these questions, closed this paper war; and I had forgotten all about the matter, when the correspondence was forwarded me, folded in official style, and indorsed at the surgeon-general's office on the back "Referred respectfully to the surgeon-in-chief ——Hospital," through whose hands alone official etiquette required all reports should pass to heads of departments. He had courteously sent it to me, and I as courteously sent it to the forwarder. Seeing that he had failed to interest the surgeon-general in the case, he drew up a statement of the affair, accusing me of disrespect (based upon the gingerbread letter particu-larly) to my *superior officer,* sending it accompanied by all the obnoxious notes to the office of the military governor of the department of Henrico, who I heard read it all with some amazement—if not interest. Back, how-ever, it came shortly again without response, and by this time some of the waggish surgeons having been made confidants in the matter, persuaded my disappointed friend to try the secretary of war; and at one of the charming breakfasts which his wife was in the habit of giving, I saw him with a smile draw from his pocket a package I knew well by that time, and made my escape just in time to avoid hearing it all over again. As I mounted the ambulance in waiting to take me to my hospital, I heard the peals of laughter that greeted the reading of those unlucky documents.

My acquaintance with my correspondent was never renewed. He kept out of my way. The only time I ever saw him again was the day he left and I viewed his pantaloons of Georgia clay embrowning the landscape adown the hill.

A better educated class of surgeons was sent to fill fortunate vacancies, and this change made my duties more agreeable. There would have been nothing disagreeable in the occupation I had assumed if a proper discretion had been exercised, or proper rules enforced, so that no demands should have been made upon the matron for that which she had no right to give. These demands were the beginning and end of my troubles; for in all else except complying with them I tried hard not to exceed the duties of my position, and succeeded so well that no temptation could induce me to interfere in any way with medical treatment, not even to offering the slightest alleviation to suffering men. During my early initiation, when quite a novice, yielding to a poor fellow's prayer for something to wash a mouth frightfully excoriated by calomel I gave him a few drops of myrrh in water, and suffered the annoyance of seeing it contemptuously tossed out of the window by the assistant surgeon. From that day I made up my mind to resist all such impulses and persevered in the same line of conduct to the end.

But antagonism was not always the rule. There were many sensible, kind-hearted efficient men among the surgeons who gave their time and talents generously to further the comfort and well-being of their patients,—men who would let me work hand in hand with them, the nurse with the doctor, and listen kindly and respectfully to my suggestions, if they were not calculated to benefit science. As I have said, the chief surgeon was an unfailing refuge in times of distress, and whenever broken down by fatigue and small miseries I sought his advice and assistance, the first was not only the very best that could be secured, but unlike most of its kind, palatable; and the last entirely efficient.

The surgeon, too, of my hospital though eccentric and wanting in decision of character, sustained my authority during sore trials as ably as he could; for the power delegated to him was not great, and his dread of responsibility a disease. He never intended to be unjust or unkind, but self-examination and investigation of characters around him was not his forte. He certainly withstood a vast amount of complaint directed against his chief matron; and while we had our pleasant little difficulties occasionally, that we still preserved amicable relations was due more to his amiable temper than my proper submission. I *think* he had many faults, but I am sure I had more, and if the popular remark which has since become a maxim, that a man must be very clever to "keep a hotel" be true, it certainly ought to apply to one who can govern a hospital.

NINE

*N*ow during the summer of 1864 began what is really meant by "war," for privations had to be endured which tried body and soul, and which temper and patience had to meet unflinchingly day and night. A growing want of confidence was forced upon the mind; and with doubts which though unexpressed were felt as to the ultimate success of our cause, there came into play the antagonistic qualities of human nature.

The money worthless, and a weak Congress and weaker financier failing to make it much more valuable than the paper it was printed on; the former refusing to the last to raise the hospital fund to meet the depreciation. Everything furnished through government contracts of the very poorest description, perhaps necessarily so from the difficulty of finding any supply.

The railroads were constantly cut so that what had been carefully collected in the country in the form of poultry and vegetables by hospital agents would be rendered unfit for use by the time the connection would be restored. The inducements for theft were great in this season of scarcity of food and clothing. The pathetic appeals made for the coarsest meal by starving men, all wore upon the health and strength of those exposed to the strain, and made life weary and hopeless. The rations became so small about this time that every ounce of flour was valuable, and there were days when it was necessary to refuse with aching heart and brimming eyes the request of decent, manly-looking fellows for a piece of dry corn-bread. If given it would have robbed the rightful owner of part of his scanty rations. After the flour or meal had been made into bread, it was almost ludicrous to see with what painful solicitude Miss G. and myself would count the rolls, or hold a council over the pans of corn-bread, measuring with a string how large we could afford to cut the squares, to be apportioned to a certain number. Sometimes when from the causes above stated, the supplies were not issued as usual, invention had to be taxed to an extreme, and every available article in our pantry brought into requisition. We had constantly to fall back upon dried apples and rice for convalescing appetites, and herb-tea and arrowroot for the very ill. There was only one way of making the last at all palatable, and that was by drenching it with whiskey. Long abstinence in the field from everything that could be considered, even then, a delicacy, had exaggerated the fancy of sick men for any particular article of food they wanted into a passion; and they begged for such peculiar dishes that surgeons and nurses might well be puzzled. The greatest difficulty in granting these desires was that tastes became contagious, and whatever one patient asked for, his neighbor and the one next to him, and so on throughout the wards, craved also, and it was impossible to decide upon whom to draw a check. No one unacquainted with our domestic relations can appreciate the difficulties under which we labored. Stoves in any degree of newness or usefulness we did not have; they were rare and expensive luxuries. As may be supposed, they were not the most convenient articles in the world to pack away in blockade-running vessels; and the trouble and expense of land transportation also seriously affected the quality of the wood for fuel, furnished us. Timber which had been condemned heretofore as unfit for use, light, soggy and decayed, became the only quality available. The bacon, too, cured the first two years of the war, when salt commanded an enormous price, in most cases was spoilt, from the economy used in preparing that article; and bacon was one of the sinews of war. We kept up brave hearts, and said we could eat the simplest fare, and wear the coarsest clothing, but there was absolutely nothing to be bought that did not rank as a luxury. It was wasting time and brain to attempt to economize, so we bent to the full force of that wise precept, "Sufficient for the day is the evil thereof." There really was a great deal of heroism displayed when looking back, at the calm courage with which I learned to count the number of mouths to be fed daily, and then contemplating the food, calculate not how much but how little each man could be satisfied with. War may be glorious in all its panoply and pride, when in the field opposing armies meet and strive for victory; but battles fought by starving the sick and wounded—by crushing in by main force day by day all the necessities of human nature, make victories hardly worth the name.

Another of my local troubles were the rats, who felt the times, and waxed strong and cunning, defying all attempts to entrap them, and skillfully levying blackmail upon us day by day, and night after night. Hunger had educated their minds and sharpened their reasoning faculties. Other vermin, the change of seasons would rid us of, but the coldest day in winter, and the hottest in summer, made no apparent difference in their vivacious strategy.

They examined traps with the air of connoisseurs, sometimes springing them from a safe position, and kicked over the bread spread with butter and strychnine to show their contempt for such underhand warfare. The men related wonderful rat-stories not well enough authenticated to put on record, but their gourmands ate all the poultices applied during the night to the sick, and dragged away the pads stuffed with bran from under the arms and legs of the wounded.

They even performed a surgical operation which would have entitled any of them to pass the board. A Virginian had been wounded in the very center of the instep of his left foot. The hole made was large, and the wound sloughed fearfully around a great lump of proud flesh which had formed in the center like an island. The surgeons feared to remove this mass, as it might be connected with the nerves of the foot, and lock-jaw might ensue. Poor Patterson would sit on his bed all day gazing at his lame foot and bathing it with a rueful face, which had brightened amazingly one morning when I paid him a visit. He exhibited it with great glee, the little island gone, and a deep hollow left, but the wound washed clean and looking healthy. Some skillful rat surgeon had done him this good service while in the search for luxuries, and he only knew that on awaking in the morning he had found the operation performed. I never had but one personal inter-view with any of them. An ancient gray gentleman, who looked a hundred years old, both in years and depravity, would eat nothing but butter, when that article was twenty dollars a pound; so finding all means of getting rid of him fail through his superior intelligence, I caught him with a fish-hook, well baited with a lump of his favorite butter, dropped into his domicile under the kitchen floor. Epicures sometimes managed to entrap them and secure a nice broil for supper, declaring that their flesh was superior to squirrel meat; but never having tasted it, I cannot add my testimony to its merits. They staid with us to the last, nor did I ever observe any signs of a desire to change their politics. Perhaps some curious *gourmet* may wish a recipe for the best mode of cooking them. The rat must be skinned, cleaned, his head cut off and his body laid open upon a square board, the legs stretched to their full extent and secured upon it with small tacks, then baste with bacon fat and roast before a good fire quickly like canvas-back ducks.

One of the remarkable features of the war was the perfect good nature with which the rebels discussed their foes. In no instance up to a certain period did I hear of any remark that savored of personal hatred. They fought for a cause and against a power, and would speak in depreciation of a corps or brigade; but "they fit us, and we fit them," was the whole story generally, and till the blowing up of the mine at Petersburgh there was a gay, insouciant style in their descriptions of the war scenes passing under their observation. But after that time the sentiment changed from an innate feeling the Southern soldiers had that mining was "a mean trick," as they expressed it. They were not sufficiently versed in military tactics to recognize that stratagem is fair in war, and what added to their indignation was the pouring in of *negro* soldiers when the breach was effected. Incensed at the surprise, they craved foes worthier of their steel, not caring to rust it in the black cloud that issued from the crater. The men had heretofore been calm and restrained, particularly before a woman, never using oaths or improper language, but the wounded that were brought in from that fight emulated the talents of Uncle Toby's army in Flanders, and eyes gleamed, and teeth clenched as they showed me the locks of their muskets to which the blood and hair still clung, when after firing, without waiting to re-load, they had clenched the barrels and fought hand to hand. If their accounts could be relied upon, it was a gallant strife and a desperate one, and ghastly wounds bore testimony of the truth of many a tale then told.

Once again the bitter blood showed itself, when, after a skirmish, the foe cut the rail track, so that the wounded could not be brought to the city. Of all the monstrous crimes that war sanctions, this is surely the most sinful. Wounded soldiers without the shelter of a roof, or the comfort of a bed of straw, left exposed to sun, dew, and rain, with hardly the prospect of a warm drink or decent food for days, knowing that comfortable quarters awaited them, all ready prepared, but rendered useless by what seems an unnecessarily cruel act. Was it any wonder that their habitual indifference to suffering gave way, and the soldier cursed loud and deep at a causeless inhumanity, which, if practiced habitually, is worse than savage? When the sufferers at last reached the hospital, their wounds had not been attended to for three days, and the sight of them was shocking.

Busy in my kitchen, seeing that the supply of necessary food was in preparation, I was spared the sight of much of the suffering, but on passing among the ambulances going in and out of the wards I descried seated up in one of them a dilapidated figure, both hands holding his head which was tied up with rags of all descriptions. He appeared to be incapable of talk-ing, but nodded and winked and made motions with head and feet. In the general confusion he had been forgotten, so I took him under my especial charge. He was taken into a ward, seated on a bed, while I stood on a bench to be able to unwind rag after rag from around his head. There was no sen-sitiveness on his part, for his eye was merry and bright, but when the last came off, what a sight!

Two balls had passed through his cheek and jaw within half an inch of each other, knocking out the teeth on both sides and cutting the tongue in half. The inflammation caused the swelling to be immense, and the absence of all previous attendance, in consequence of the detention of the wounded until the road could be mended, had aggravated the symptoms. There was nothing fatal to be apprehended, but fatal wounds are not always the most trying. The sight of this was the most sickening my long experience had ever seen. The swollen lips turned out, and the mouth filled with blood, matter, fragments of teeth from amidst all of which the maggots in countless numbers swarmed and writhed, while the smell generated by this putridity was unbearable. Castile soap and soft sponges soon cleansed the offensive cavity, and he was able in an hour to swallow some nourishment he drew through a quill. The following morning I found him reading the newspaper, and entertaining every one about him by his abortive attempts to make himself understood, and in a week he actually succeeded in doing so. The first request distinctly enunciated was that he wanted a looking-glass to see if his sweetheart would be willing to kiss him when she saw him. We all assured him that she would not be worthy of the name if she would not be delighted to do so.

An order came about this time to clear out the lower wards for the reception of improperly-vaccinated patients, who soon after arrived in great numbers. They were dreadfully afflicted objects, many of them with sores so deep and thick upon arms and legs that amputation had to be resorted to, to preserve life. As fast as the eruption would be healed in one spot, it would break out in another, for the blood seemed entirely poisoned. The unfortunate victims bore the infliction as they had borne everything else painful—with calm patience and indifference to suffering. Sometimes a favorable comparison would be made between this and the greater loss of limbs. No one who was a daily witness to their agonies from this cause, can help feeling indignant at charges made of inhumanity to Federal prisoners of war, who were vaccinated with the same virus; and while on this subject, though it may be outside of the recollections of hospital life, I cannot help stating that on no occasion was the question of rations and medicines to be issued for Federal prisoners discussed in my presence; and circumstances placed me where I had the best opportunity of hearing the truth (living with the wife of a Cabinet officer); that good evidence was not given, that the Confederate commissary-general, by order of the government issued to them the same rations it gave its soldiers in the field, and only when reductions of food had to be made in our army, were they also made in the prisons. The question of supplies for them was an open and a vexed one among the people generally, and angry and cruel things were *said;* but every one cognizant of facts in Richmond *knows* that even when General Lee's army lived on corn-meal at times that the prisoners still received their usual rations. At a cabinet meeting when the Commissary-General [Northrop] advocated putting the prisoners on the half rations which our soldiers had been obliged to content themselves with for some time, Gen. Lee opposed him on the ground that men animated by companionship and active service could be satisfied with less than prisoners with no hope and leading an inactive life. Mr. Davis sided with him, and the question was settled that night, although in his anger Mr. Northrop accused Gen. Lee of showing this consideration because his son was a prisoner in the enemy's lines.

Ten

My hospital was now entirely composed of Virginians and Marylanders, and the nearness to the homes of the former entailed upon me an increase of care in the shape of wives, sisters, cousins, aunts, and whole families including the historic baby at the breast. They came in troops, and hard as it was to know how to dispose of them, it was harder to send them away. Sometimes they brought their provisions with them, but not often, and even when they did there was no place for them to cook their food. It must be remembered that everything was reduced to the lowest minimum, even fuel. They could not remain all day in the wards with men around them, and if even they were so willing, the restraint on wounded, restless patients who wanted to throw their limbs about with freedom during hot summer days, was unbearable.

Generally their only idea of kindness was giving sick men what food they would take in any quantity and of every quality, and in the furtherance of their views they were pugnacious in the extreme. Whenever rules circumscribed their plans they abused the government, then the hospital and then myself. Many ludicrous incidents happened daily, and I have often laughed heartily at seeing the harassed ward-master heading away a pertinacious female who failing to get past him at one door would try the three others perseveringly. They seemed to think it a pious and patriotic duty not to be afraid or ashamed under *any* circumstances. One sultry day I found a whole family accompanied by two young lady friends seated around a wounded man's bed; as I passed through six hours later, they held the same position.

"Had not you all better go home?" I said goodnaturedly.

"We came to see my cousin," answered one very crossly. "He is wounded."

"But you have been with him all morning, and that is a restraint upon the other men. Come again to-morrow."

A consultation was held, but when it ceased no movement was made, the older ones only lighting their pipes and smoking in silence.

"Will you come back to-morrow, and go now?"

"No! You come into the wards when you please, and so will we!"

"But it is my duty to do so. Besides, I always ask permission to enter, and never stay longer than fifteen minutes at a time."

Another unbroken silence, which was a trial to any patience left, and finding no movement made, I handed some clothing to a patient near.

"Here is a clean shirt and drawers for you, Mr. Wilson; put them on as soon as I get out of the ward."

I had hardly reached my kitchen, when the whole procession, pipes and all, passed me solemnly and angrily; but for many days, and even weeks, there was no ridding the place of this large family connection. Their sins were manifold. They overfed their relative who was recovering from an attack of typhoid fever, and even defiantly seized the food for the purpose from under my very nose. They marched on me *en masse* at ten o'clock at night, with a requisition from the boldest for sleeping quarters. The steward was summoned, and said "he didn't keep a hotel," so in a weak moment of pity for their desolate state, I imprudently housed them in my laundry. They entrenched themselves there for six days, making predatory incursions into my kitchen during my temporary absences, ignoring Miss G. completely. The object of their solicitude recovered and was sent to the field, and finding my writs of ejectment were treated with contemptuous silence, I sought an explanation. The same spokeswoman alluded to above, met me half-way. She said a battle was imminent she had heard, and she had determined to remain, as her husband might be wounded. In the ensuing press of business she was forgotten, and strangely enough, her husband was brought in with a bullet in his neck the following week. The back is surely fitted to the burden, so I contented myself with retaking my laundry, and letting her shift for herself, while a whole month slipped away. One morning my arrival was greeted with a general burst of merriment from everybody I met, white and black. Experience had made me sage, and my first question was a true shot, right in the center.

"Where is Mrs. Daniells?" (she who had always been spokeswoman).

"In ward G. She has sent for you two or three times."

"What is the matter now?"

"You must go and see."

There was something going on, either amusing or amiss. I entered ward G, and walked up to Daniells' bed. One might have heard a pin drop.

I had supposed, up to this time, that I had been called upon to bear and suffer every annoyance that humanity and the state of the country could inflict; but here was something most unexpected in addition; for lying composedly on her husband's cot (he had relinquished it for the occasion) lay Mrs. Daniells, and her baby, just two hours old.

The conversation that ensued is not worth repeating, being more of the nature of soliloquy. The poor little wretch had ventured into a bleak and comfortless portion of the world, and its inhuman mother had not provided a rag to cover it. No one could scold her at such a time, however ardently they might desire to do so. But what was to be done? I went in search of my chief surgeon, and our conversation although didactic was hardly satisfactory on the subject.

"Doctor, Mrs. Daniells has a baby. She is in ward G. What shall I do with her?"

"A baby! Bless me! Ah indeed! You must get it some clothes."

"What must I do with *her?*"

"Move her to an empty ward and give her some tea and toast."

This was offered, but Mrs. D. said she would wait until dinner-time and have some bacon and greens.

The baby was a sore annoyance. The ladies of Richmond made up a wardrobe, each contributing some article, and at the end of the month, Mrs. D., the child, and a basket of clothing and provisions were sent to the cars with a return ticket to her home in western Virginia. My feelings of relief can be imagined. But the end had not come. An hour after the ambulance had started with them, it stopped at my kitchen door apparently empty, and the black driver with a grin half of delighted mischief and half of fear silently lifted a bundle out and deposited it carefully upon my kitchen dresser. Mrs. Daniells' baby!

The unnatural woman had deserted it, leaving it in the railroad depot, but the father fortunately was still with us and to him I appealed. A short furlough was obtained for him, and he was despatched home with his embarrassing charge and a quart of milk. He was a wretched picture of helplessness, but had I sent again for the mother I should never have got rid of her. It may be remarked *en passant* that she was not wholly ungrateful, for the baby was named after me.

There were no means of keeping the relations of patients from coming to them. There had been rules made to meet their invasion, but it was impossible to carry them out, as in the instance of a wife wanting to remain with her husband; and besides even the better class of people looked upon the comfort and care of a hospital as a farce. They resented the detention there of men who in many instances could lie in bed and point to their homes within sight, and argued that they would have better attention and food if allowed to go to their families. That *maladie du pays* called commonly nostalgia, the home-sickness which wrings the heart and impoverishes the blood, killed many a brave soldier; and the matron who day by day had to stand helpless and powerless by the bed of the sufferer, knowing that a week's furlough would make his heart sing for joy, and save his wife from widow-hood, learned the most bitter lesson of endurance that could be taught.

This home-sickness recognized no palliation. However carefully the appetite might be pampered, or stimulants prepared and given, the food never nourished, the drink never strengthened; the decay would be gradual, but death was inevitable. Perhaps when recovery seemed hopeless, a statement of the case might procure a furlough from the examining board of surgeons, but the patient would then be too weak and low to profit by the concession. It was wonderful to see how long the poor broken machine would hold out in some cases. For months I have watched a victim, helpless, hopeless and motionless, simply receive into his mouth daily a few spoonfuls of nourishment, making no other movement, the skin barely covering the bones, and the skeleton of the face as sharply defined as it might have been days after dissolution. The answer to cheering words seldom exceeding a slight movement of the eyelids. Towards the end of the war, this detention of men who could have been furloughed at first, and some other abuses were reformed by allowing a board to be convened of three of the oldest surgeons attached to the hospital, who had authority to dispose of such cases without deferring to higher powers. There had been so much imposition practiced by men desirous of getting furloughs, and so many abuses had crept in despite the stringency of rules, that severity seemed necessary.

ELEVEN

$\mathcal{T}$he spring campaign of 1864 again opened with the usual "On to Richmond." Day after day and night after night would the sudden explosion of cannon boom upon the air. The enemy were always coming, and curiosity seemed to have usurped the place of fear among the women. In the silence of night the alarm bells would suddenly peal out, till the order to ring them at any sign of danger was modified to a command to sound them only in case of positive attack. The people became so accustomed to the report of fire-arms, that they scarcely interrupted their conversation at corners of the streets to ask in what direction the foe was advancing, or if there was any foe at all.

There was such entire reliance upon the military vigilance that guarded the city, and former attacks had been so promptly repelled, that whatever was ultimately to be the result of the war, no one trembled then for Richmond. So the summer of 1864 passed, and early in September our hearts were gladdened by the tidings that the exchange of prisoners was to be renewed. The sick and wounded of our hospital (but few in number just then) were transferred to other quarters, and the wards put in order to receive our men from Northern prisons.

Can any pen or pencil do justice to those squalid pictures of famine and desolation? Those gaunt, lank skeletons with the dried yellow flesh clinging to bones enlarged by dampness and exposure? Those pale, bluish lips and feverish eyes, glittering and weird when contrasted with the famine-stricken faces,—that flitting, piteous, scared smile which greeted their fellow creatures, all will live forever before the mental vision that then witnessed it.

Living and dead were taken from the flag-of-truce boat, not distinguishable save from the difference of care exercised in moving them. The Federal prisoners we had released were in many instances in a like state, but our ports had been blockaded, our harvests burned, our cattle stolen, our country wasted. Even had we felt the desire to succor, where could the wherewithal have been found? But the foe,—the ports of the world were open to him. He could have fed his prisoners upon milk and honey, and not have missed either. When we review the past, it would seem that Christianity was but a name—that the Atonement had failed, and Christ had lived and died in vain.

But it was no time then for vague reflections. With beating heart, throbbing head and icy hands I went among this army of martyrs and spectres whom it was almost impossible to recognize as human beings; powerless to speak to them, choking with unavailing pity, but still striving to aid and comfort. There was but little variety of appearance. From bed to bed the same picture met the eye. Hardly a vestige of human appearance left.

The passion of sympathy could only impede my efforts if yielded to, for my hand shook too tremulously even to allow me to put the small morsels of bread soaked in wine into their mouths. It was all we dared to give at first. Some lay as if dead with limbs extended, but the greater part had drawn up their knees to an acute angle, a position they never changed until they died. Their more fortunate comrades said that the attitude was generally assumed, as it reduced the pangs of hunger and relieved the craving that gnawed them by day and by night. The Federal prisoners may have been starved at the South, we cannot deny the truth of the charge, in many instances; but we starved with them; we had only a little to share with any—but the subject had better be left to die in silence.

One among them lingered in patience the usual three days that appeared to be their allotted space of life on their return. He was a Marylander, Richard Hammond Key, grandson of Francis Barton [*sic*] Key, author of "The Star-Spangled Banner," and hence, heir to a name renowned in the history of his country, the last of seven sons reared in affluence, but presenting the same bluish, bloodless appearance common to them all. Hoping that there would be some chance of his rallying, I gave him judicious nursing and good brandy. Every precaution was taken, but the third day fever supervened and the little life left waned rapidly. He gave me the trinkets cut from gutta percha buttons that he had beguiled his captivity in making at Point Lookout, to send to his family, handing me one of them for a souvenir; begged that he might be buried apart from the crowd in some spot where those who knew and cared for him might find him some day, and quietly slept himself to death that night. The next morning was the memorable 29th September, 1864, when the enemy made a desperate and successful attack, taking Fort Harrison, holding it and placing Richmond in jeopardy for four hours. The alarm bells summoned the citizens together, and the shops being closed to allow those who kept them to join the city guards, there were no means of buying a coffin, or getting a hearse. It was against the rules to keep a body beyond a certain time on the hospital grounds, so little time was to be lost if I intended keeping my promise to the dead. I summoned a convalescent carpenter from one of the wards, made him knock together a rough coffin from some loose boards, and taking the seats out of my ambulance had it, with the body enclosed, put in. My driver was at his post with the guards, so taking the reins and kneeling in the little space at the side of the coffin I started for Hollywood cemetery, a distance of five miles.

The enemy were then in sight, and from every elevated point the masses of manoeuvering soldiers and flash of the enemy's cannon could be distinguished. Only stopping as I passed through the city to buy a piece of ground from the old cemetery agent, I reached Hollywood by twelve o'clock. Near the burying ground I met the Rev. Mr. [J. D.] McCabe, requested his presence and assistance, and we stood side by side while the sexton dug his grave. The rain was pouring in torrents, while the clergyman repeated the Episcopal burial service from memory. Besides ourselves there [were] but two poor women, of the humblest class of life—Catholics, who passing casually, dropped upon their knees, undeterred by the rain, and paid their humble tribute of respect to the dead. He had all the honors of a soldier's burial paid to him unconsciously, for the cannon roared and the musketry rattled, mingling with the thunder and lightning of Heaven's artillery. The sexton held his hat over the small piece of paper on which I inscribed his name and birthplace (to be put on his headboard) to protect it from the rain, and with a saddened heart for the solitary grave we left behind I drove back to the city. The reverend gentleman was left at his home, and, perhaps, to this day does not know who his companion was during that strange hour. I found the city in the same state of excitement, for no authentic news was to be heard, or received, except perhaps at official quarters; and it was well known that we had no troops nearer than Petersburg, save the citizens who had enrolled themselves for defense; therefore, too anxious to return directly to the hospital, I drove to the residence of one of the cabinet ministers, where I was engaged to attend a dinner, and found the mistress of the establishment, surrounded by her servants and trunks preparing for a hasty retreat when necessary. Some persuasion induced her to desist, and the situation of the house commanding an extensive view of the surrounding country, we watched the advance of the enemy from the extreme northeast, for with the aid of opera-glasses we could even distinguish the colors of their uniforms. Slowly onward moved the bodies of dark blue, emerging from and disappearing into the woods, seeming to be skirting around them, but not to be diminishing the distance between, although each moment becoming more distinct, which proved their advance, while not one single Confederate jacket could be observed over the whole sweep of ground.

Half an anxious hour passed, and then, far away against the distant horizon, one single mounted horseman emerged from a thick wood, looked cautiously around, passed across the road and disappeared. He was in gray, and followed by another and another, winding around and cutting off the foe. Then a startling peal at the bell, and a courier brought the news that Wade Hampton and his cavalry were close upon the rear of the enemy. There was no occasion for fear after this, for General Hampton was the Montrose of the Southern army, he who could make any cause famous with his pen and glorious with his sword. The dinner continued in course of preparation, and was seasoned, when served, by spirits brightened by the strong reaction.

TWELVE

*T*he horrors that attended, in past times, the bombardment of a city, were experienced in a great degree in Richmond during the fighting around us. The close proximity to the scenes of strife, the din of battle, the bursting of shells, the fresh wounds of the men hourly brought in were daily occurrences. Walking through the streets during this time, after the duties of the hospital were over, when night had well advanced, the pavement around the railroad depot would be crowded with wounded men just brought in, and laid there waiting for conveyance to the receiving hospitals. Some on stretchers, others on the bare bricks, or laid on a thin blanket, suffering from wounds hastily wrapped around with strips of coarse, unbleached, galling bandages of homespun cotton, on which the blood had congealed and stiffened until every crease cut like a knife. Women passing accidentally, like myself, would put down their basket or bundle, and ringing at the bell of neighboring houses, ask for basin and soap, warm water, and a few soft rags, and going from sufferer to sufferer, try to alleviate with what skill they possessed, the pain of fresh wounds, change the uneasy posture, and allay the thirst. Others would pause and look on, till the labor appearing to require no particular talent, they too would follow the example set them, and occasionally asking a word of advice, do their duty carefully and willingly. Idle boys would get a pine knot or tallow-dip, and stand quietly and curiously as torch-bearers, till the scene, with its gathering accessories formed a strange picture, not easily forgotten. Persons driving in different vehicles would alight sometimes in evening dress, and choosing the wounded most in need of surgical aid, put them in their places, and send them to their destination, continuing their way on foot. There was little conversation carried on, no necessity for introductions, and no names ever asked or given. This indifference to personality was a peculiarity strongly exhibited in hospitals, for after nursing a sick or wounded patient for months, he has often left without any curiosity exhibited as regarded my name, my whereabouts, or indeed any thing connected with me. A case in point was related by a friend. When the daughter of our general had devoted much time and care to a sick man in one of the hospitals, he seemed to feel so little gratitude for the attention paid, that her companion to rouse him told him that Miss Lee was his nurse. "Lee, Lee?" he said.

"There are some Lees down in Mississippi who keep a tavern there. Is she one of them Lees?"

Almost of the same style, although a little worse was the remark of one of my sick, a poor fellow who had been wounded in the head and who, though sensible enough ordinarily, would feel the effect of the sun on his brain when exposed to its influence. After advising him to wear a wet paper doubled into the crown of his hat more from a desire to show some interest in him than from any belief in its efficacy, I paused at the door long enough to hear him ask the ward-master "who that was?" "Why, that is the matron of the hospital; she gives you all the food you eat, and attends to things." "Well!" said he, "I always did think this government was a confounded sell and now I am sure of it, when they put such a little fool to manage such a big hospital as this."

The ingenuity of the men was wonderful in making toys and trifles, and a great deal of mechanical talent was developed by the enforced inaction of hospital life. Every ward had its draught-board and draughtsmen cut out of hard wood and stained with vegetable dies, and sometimes chessmen would be cut out with a common knife, in such ornamentation that they would not have disgraced a drawing-room. One man carved pipes from ivy root, with exquisitely-cut shields on the bowls, bearing the arms of the different states and their mottoes. He would charge and easily get a hundred and fifty dollars for a pipe (Confederate paper was then sixty cents for the dollar), and he only used his well-worn pocket-knife. Playing cards—the greatest comfort to alleviate the tedium of their sick life—were difficult to get a substitute for, so that the original packs had a hard time. They became, as may be supposed from the hands which used them, very dirty in a short time, and the corners in a particularly disreputable condition, but after the diffusion of the Oxford editions of the different books of the Bible sent from England as a donation, the soldiers took a lesson, and rounded the corners in imitation. A pack of cards after four years' use in a Southern hospital was beyond criticism.

The men had their fashions, too, sometimes insisting upon having light blue pants drawn for them, and at other seasons preferring gray; but while the mania for either color raged, they would be dissatisfied with the other.

When the quartermaster-general issued canvas shoes, there was a loud dissatisfaction expressed in constant grumbling, till some original genius dyed the whitish tops by the liberal application of poke-berries. He was the Brummel of the day, and for many months crimson shoes were the rage, and long rows of unshod men would sit under the eaves of the wards, all diligently employed in the same labor and up to their elbows in red juice.

This fashion died out, and gave place to a button mania. Men who had never had a dream or a hope beyond a horn convenience to keep their clothing together, saved up their scanty means to replace them with gilt, and made neat little wooden shelves with a slit through the middle into which the buttons slid, so that they could be cleaned and brightened without taking them off, or soiling the jacket. With the glitter of buttons came the corresponding taste for gilt bands and tinsel around the battered hat, so that while our future was lowering darker and darker, our soldiers were amusing themselves like children who had no interest in the coming results.

～

The duty which of all others pressed most heavily upon me and which I never did perform voluntarily was that of telling a man he could not live, when he was perhaps unconscious that there was any danger apprehended from his wound. The idea of death so seldom occurs when disease and suffering have not wasted the frame and destroyed the vital energies, that there is but little opening or encouragement to commence such a subject unless the patient suspects the result ever so slightly. In many cases, too, the yearning for life was so strong that to destroy the hope was beyond human power. Life was for him a furlough, family and friends once more around him; a future was all he wanted, and considered it cheaply purchased if only for a month by the endurance of any wound, however painful or wearisome.

There were long discussions among those responsible during the war, as to the advisability of the frequent amputations on the field, and often when a hearty, fine-looking man in the prime of life would be brought in minus an arm or leg, I would feel as if it might have been saved, but experience taught me the wisdom of prompt measures. Poor food and great exposure had thinned the blood and broken down the system so entirely that secondary amputations performed in the hospital almost invariably resulted in death, after the second year of the war. The blood lost on the battlefield when the wound was first received would enfeeble the already impaired system and render it incapable of further endurance.

Once we received a strong, stalwart soldier from Alabama, and after five days' nursing, finding the inflammation from the wound in his arm too great to save the limb, the attending surgeon requested me to feed him on the best I could command; by that means to try and give him strength to undergo amputation. Irritability of stomach as well as indifference to food always accompanying gun-shot wounds, it was necessary, while the fever continued, to give him as much nourishment in as small a compass as possible, as well as easily digestible food, that would assimilate with his enfeebled condition. Beef tea he (in common with all soldiers and I believe men) would not, or could not take, or anything I suggested as an equivalent, so getting his consent to drink some "chemical mixture," I prepared the infusion. Chipping up a pound of beef and pouring upon it a half pint of water, the mixture was stirred until all the blood was extracted, and only a teaspoonful of white fibre remained; a little salt was added, and favored by the darkness of the corner of the ward in which he lay, I induced him to swallow it. He drank without suspicion, and fortunately liked it, only complaining of its being too sweet; and by the end of ten days his pulse was fairly good, and there had been no accession of fever. Every precaution was taken, both for his sake and the benefit of the experiment, and the arm taken off by the most skillful surgeon we had. After the amputation, which he bore bravely, he looked as bright and well as before, and so on for five days—then the usual results followed. The system proved not strong enough to throw out the "pus" or inflammation; and this, mingling with the blood, produced that most fatal of all diseases, pyæmia, from which no one ever recovers.

He was only one of numerous cases, so that my heart beat twice as rapidly as ordinarily whenever there were any arrangements progressing for amputation, after any length of time had elapsed since the wound, or any effort made to save the limb. The only cases under my observation that survived were two Irishmen, and it was really so difficult to kill an Irishman that there was little cause for boasting on the part of the officiating surgeons. One of them had his leg cut off in pieces, amputation having been performed three times, and the last heard from him was that he had married a young wife and settled on a profitable farm she owned in Macon, Georgia.

He had touched the boundary lines of the "unknown land," had been given up by the surgeons, who left me with orders to stimulate him if possible. The priest (for he was a Catholic) was naturally averse to my disturbing what he considered the last moments of a dying man who had made his confession and taken his farewell of this world, and which ought to have been devoted to less worldly temptations than mint juleps; and a rather brisk encounter was the result of a difference of opinion on the subject; for if he was responsible for the soul, so was I for the body, and I held my ground firmly.

It was hard for an Irishman and a good Catholic to have to choose at this supreme moment between religion and whiskey; but though his head was turned respectfully towards good Father T —— his eyes rested too lovingly on the goblet offered to his lips to allow me to make any mistake as to the results of his ultimate intentions. The interpretation put by me on that look was that Callahan thought that as long as first proof brandy and mint lasted in the Confederacy this world was good enough for him, and the result proved that I was not mistaken. He always gave me the credit I have awarded to the juleps, and until the evacuation of Richmond kept me informed of his domestic happiness.

Thirteen

*T*hough my health up to this time had withstood the bad effects of exposure and exertion, the strain had become too great, and the constantly recurring agitation which had been excited each day on receiving the returned prisoners, had broken me down completely. A visit to the surgeon-general with a request for a month's leave of absence, met with a ready acquiescence. The old gentleman was very urbane, even making one or two grim jokes, and handed me not only permission to leave, but the necessary transportation. Very necessary in this case, as traveling expenses were enormously high, and the government had seized for the whole month of October the railroads for military use, putting a complete stop to private travel.

It had been like tearing body and soul apart, when necessity compelled me to leave my hospital, from which I had never been separated but one day in nearly four years; and when all arrangements for departure had been completed, Miss G. urged, entreated and commanded to keep a sharp look-out upon the whiskey, and be alike impenetrable to feints, strategems and entreaties, my heart began to sink. A visit to the wards did not tend to strengthen my wavering resolves. The first invalid to whom I communicated the news of my intended departure burst into a passion of tears, and improved my frame of mind by requesting me to kill him at once, for he would certainly die if left. Standing by his bedside, unsettled and irresolute, all the details of my daily life rose before me. The early and comforting visit to the sick after their feverish, restless night; when even if there were no good to be effected, they would feel the kindness, and every man's head would be thrust out of the bed-clothes as by one impulse, and jealousy evinced when a longer pause by one bedside than another would arouse the feeling. Often has the ward-master recalled me when at the distance of a quarter of a mile from his ward, at the request of a patient, and when going back to find out what was wanted, a hearty convalescent would explain that I had passed through and omitted to speak to him.

Farewells were exchanged at last, and the 6th October, 1864, found me at the Fredericksburg station, *en route* for Georgia. A search at the last moment before stepping into the cars, discovered that my keys, together with my watch, had been left at the hospital, while, as an equivalent, there remained at the bottom of my basket half a salt mackerel (a rare luxury in the Confederacy), begged for a sick man who fancied it, a day before, and forgotten in the hurry of packing. I was compelled to defer my start until the 7th.

There are some schoolday recollections hanging around the softening by Hannibal of a rugged journey by the plentiful application of vinegar; but what acid could soften the rigors of that trip to Georgia? They can hardly be recounted in any degree of limited space. With the aid of two gentlemen, and indeed every disengaged man on the road, a safe termination was effected after many days, and a delicious holiday passed in idleness and *Confederate* luxury, free from the wear and tear of constantly excited feelings. Then came the stern reflection that I had no right to exceed the furlough of thirty days accorded by Dr. Moore. A search was immediately made for an escort, which having failed, general advice was unanimously given to "go alone," on the grounds that women had become entirely independent at this time, and "no man knowing the object of your journey could fail to give you all the assistance you would need."

Fired with this Quixotic sentiment, an early start was made. Finding almost immediately that I had not received checks for my trunks, I ventured, while the afflatus lasted, to touch a man who sat in front of me on the arm, and request him to call the conductor. "I am sorry to say that I am not acquainted with him," was the answer; and down I went to zero, never rising again till my journey was accomplished.

Perhaps the details of my trials may give my readers some idea of the state of the country at that time. At West Point, which took an hour and a half's travel to reach from Lagrange, we had to sleep all night, there being no connection for twelve hours. There were no bed-rooms, and no candles to be had, and the female travelers sat in the little bar of the tavern (the leading hotel being closed) brightened by a pine knot, with their feet on the sanded floor, and ate what they had provided themselves with from their baskets.

Another two hours' travel on to Opelika the next day, and another detention for half-a-dozen hours. At Columbus, a rumor that the cars had been seized for government transportation made me anxious concerning the nature of my ticket, which I found to my dismay was not suited to meet the emergency through some inadvertence; so long before starting-time I

was waiting at the depot seated on my trunk, half amused and half morti-
fied at the resemblance thus offered to an emigrant Irish servant woman.
The place was crowded with invalided soldiers, for the government was
moving the hospitals to the lower part of the state, and idle spectators seeing my evident alarm offered all kinds of irrational advice. A suggestion was
sensibly made by some one that by seeking one of the most helpless of the
wounded and requesting him to allow me to pass as his nurse my object
might be effected; but every man to whom I opened my proposals seemed
alarmed at and opposed to this idea. Towards the last the confusion became
distracting—everybody calling for the conductor, who possessing no
power, the cars being under military control, first denied his identity and
then hid himself.

Help came at the last moment in the form of a red-faced, half-tipsy Irish
porter who had been cheering me on with winks of encouragement at my
frantic efforts for some time. "Lit me put yer trunks on," he said, and "thin
go to Colonel Frankland at the rare of the cars—sure he's the man to help
the faymales."

My forlorn hope, Colonel Frankland, was standing on the platform at
the extreme rear of the cars, surrounded by a semi-circle below, about
twenty-five feet deep, all pressing on to get to seats already too full. He was
gesticulating and shouting like a madman. The lame, the halt, and the blind
stood around. Crutches, splints, and huge sticks represented a small wood.
Green blinds over eyes, raw faces peeled from erysipelas, and still showing
variegated hues of iodine, gave picturesqueness to the scene. Had he borne
Caesar and his fortunes he could not have been more interested. For two
hours he had been stemming this living tide.

I had met and fraternized with a lady and gentleman, old acquaintances,
encountered at the depot, who appeared as anxious to get Northward as
myself; so telling her not to move until I had either achieved my object or
failed, and if I made her a sign to join me, I took my position at the fag end
of the crowd below the colonel, and undeterred by distance and uproar I
essayed a faint call for notice. The sound died away in my throat, but my
Irish friend (I am sure he took me for one of his cousins from the "ould
counthrie") was by my side in an instant and repeated the call. A hundred
voices took up the refrain, "A lady wants to speak to the colonel," and uni-
versal curiosity regarding the *private* nature of my business being exhibited
by a profound silence I raised my voice as Mause Headrigg said, "like a pelican

in the wilderness: "Colonel Frankland, I must get forward on this train tonight. Government business requires me to be in Richmond by the 1st November."

"Can't do it, Madam. Would like to oblige you, but can't go against my orders. The cars are for the use of sick and wounded soldiers alone."

"But Colonel Frankland, hundreds of invalids are waiting for their breakfast, dinner and supper in Richmond. I am the matron of —— hospital."

"Can't help it, Madam! If you men there don't keep away from this platform and leave a passage way, I'll put the front rank under arrest!"

"Oh! Colonel Frankland, cannot I stand on the platform, if I am not allowed to use the cars?"

"No, Madam, it would be dangerous. Sorry to refuse."

"Let me go in the freight train."

"There is no freight train."

"Well, the box cars? I take very little room."

"They are crowded, Madam, crowded. Keep off, men, keep off there!"

The steam blew and whistled fearfully and the bell clanged an uproar of sound. A passing car came rushing by and my courage was oozing fast. "Try him agin!" said my Irish friend, who unable to get near me, shouted his secret.

"Oh! Colonel Frankland, excuse my pertinacity, but what *can* I do? Let me go on in the mail car! I will not even open my eyes to look at the outside of the letters."

"Against the law. Cannot be done. How can I infringe upon my orders? Will no one keep those confounded men off?"

"I *will,* Colonel Frankland, if you will let me get up by your side. I will keep every single man away. Now men, keep off, I beg of you, for I must get to Richmond, and moreover, I wear very long hair-pins."

"Thank you, Madam, thank you. Now men, you hear what this lady says, and I know she will be as good as her word." A hundred hands helped me up. I looked for my friend, the red-nosed Irishman, but he was gone. Another moment and my friend stood by my side, assisted by the Irishman, who tipped me a comprehensive wink which set my mind at rest as regarded the safety of my trunk.

"This is not fair," said the Colonel. "You promised that no one should get on."

"Oh, no, I promised that not a *single man* should do so. This is a woman.

Will you let her husband join her? He is not a *single* man, for he has a wife and nine children!"

The result may be imagined. Our party, very much relieved, were soon inside, where we found four comfortable seats reserved for General Beauregard and staff, which were unoccupied from these gentlemen being detained at Macon.

At that city, where we were compelled to pass the night, the same state of things existed, and with depressed spirits I drove to the cars to see if any arrangement could be effected by which I could pursue my journey. The road would not be opened to the traveling public for a month, so an effort had to be made. An appeal to the authorities resulted as I expected, in defeat, so I again tried my manoeuver of trying to interest subordinates.

Failing, however, and baffled at every turn, while sitting again upon my trunk, the mail agent, standing in the doorway of his car, caught my eye. Improving the opportunity, I commenced a conversation, ending in an insinuating appeal to be taken into the mail box. Success and installation in his little square domicile followed, and my friend, passing out without any explanation, locked the door on the outside. There were no windows and no light whatever; the hour six in the evening. Seated in loneliness and darkness till the town clock struck eight, every fear that could arise in the brain of a silly woman assailed me. Did the train I was in go to Augusta, and if not, would I be left where I was all night? Was the man who locked me up the mail agent? If he came back and robbed and murdered me, would any one ever miss me? Having had nothing to eat but a couple of biscuits in twenty-four hours, and my brain being, in consequence, proportionately light, imagination seized the reins from common sense, which fled in the presence of utter darkness and loneliness.

At last the key turned in the lock, and the light of a lantern dispelled some of my terrors. The cars started and the agent commenced sorting his letters, first bolting us in securely. A couple of hours passed and my mind was gradually losing its tone of unpleasant doubt as to the wisdom of my proceedings, when my busy companion knocked off work and essayed to play the agreeable. He was communicative in the extreme, giving me his biography, which proved him to be a Connecticut man, and very much dissatisfied with the Confederacy, particularly with the state of the money market. So long as he kept to his personal recollections all was right, but he soon claimed a return of confidence, and grew hourly more patronizing and conversational. His tone and manner, the loneliness of the position, and the impossibility of any fortunate interruption occurring becoming unbearable at last, there is no knowing what I might have ventured to do, in the way of breaking out, if the cars had not fortunately run off the track. On we bumped, happily on level ground, for two minutes or more; the engineer entirely unconscious of the fact and no way of communicating with him, as the soldiers were lying over the rope on the top of the cars, so that pulling was in vain. At last a pause, and then a crowd, and then a familiar name was called, most welcome to my ears. I repeated it aloud until the owner was by my side, and the rest of the night was spent in asking questions and receiving information. At daylight he left me to rejoin his command, while we continued on to Augusta.

As usual, when we arrived there no vehicle of any kind met us at the depot. Since I was the only woman in the cars, the mail driver offered me a seat upon the mail-bags, and as it was raining I accepted, and in this August style reached the hotel by breakfast time. All military suspension ceased here, but there was detention for two hours, and this was enlivened by an amusing episode at the depot.

Directly in front of me sat an old Georgia up-country woman, placidly regarding the box cars full of men on the parallel rails, waiting like ourselves to start. She knitted and gazed, and at last inquired "who was them ar soldiers, and whar was they a-going to?" The information that they were Yankee prisoners startled her considerably. The knitting ceased abruptly (all the old women in the Southern States knitted socks for the soldiers while traveling), and the Cracker bonnet of dark brown homespun was thrown back violently, for her whole nervous system seemed to have received a galvanic shock. Then she caught her breath with a long gasp, lifted on high her thin, trembling hand, accompanied by the trembling voice, and made them a speech:

"Ain't you ashamed of you-uns," she piped, "a-coming down here a-spiling our country, and a-robbing our henroosts? What did we ever do to you-uns that you should come a-killing our brothers and sons? Ain't you ashamed of you-uns? What for do you want us to live with you-uns, you poor white trash? I ain't got a single nigger that would be so mean as to force himself where he warn't wanted, and what do we-uns want with you?

Ain't you—" but here came a roar of laughter from both cars, and shaking with excitement the old lady pulled down her spectacles, which in the excitement she had pushed up on her forehead, and tried in vain to resume her labors with uncertain fingers.

From here to Richmond there occurred the usual detentions and trials of railroad travel under the existing circumstances. The windows of the cars were broken out in many places. Sometimes no fire for want of stoves, and the nights damp and chilly. All in utter darkness, for the lamps were gone, and could they have been replaced, there would have been no oil.

We crawled along, stopping every hour almost, to tinker up some part of the car or the road, getting out at times when the conductor announced that the travelers must walk "a spell or two," meaning from one to five miles. Crowds of women were getting in and out all the way, the male passengers grumbling aloud that "women had better stay at home, they had no business to be running around in such times." This was said so often that it became very unpleasant, till the tables were turned early one morning at Gainsborough, when a large-sized female made her way along the center of the car, looking from right to left in the vain search for a seat. None being vacant, she stopped short, and addressed the astonished male passengers with more vigor than elegance: "What for pity sake do you men mean by running all around the country for, instead of staying in the field, as you ought to do? You keep filling up the cars so that a woman can't attend to her business. Your place should be opposite the enemy." This diversion on our behalf was received silently, but many seats were soon vacated by their occupants on the plea of "taking a little smoke."

At last, the 1st of November found me weary, hungry, cold and exhausted by travel at the Richmond depot, four hours after schedule time; with that most terrible scourge, a bad, nervous headache racking me all over. The crowd around was immense, so that by the time it opened and dispersed sufficiently to let me make my way through, every vehicle had left, if there had ever been any there before. As usual, my telegram had not been received, so there was no one to meet me, and pain rendering me indifferent to appearances I quietly spread my shawl upon a bench and myself upon it.

For how long I cannot say, but I was roused by a voice asking what I wanted, and what was the matter? "Any kind of a vehicle to take me home," was the answer. After a few moments' delay my new friend returned with the information that there was only a market cart, which if I was willing to ride in, was for hire. If it had been a hearse it would have been hailed with welcome. My two trunks were put on, and I was deposited on them. The hour, eleven at night.

I looked first at the horse. He had a shadowy gray skin stretched over his prominent bones, and in the dim, misty light, seemed a mere phantom. The driver next came under observation. A little dried-up, gray black, old darkey, with a brown rag tied around his head, but like all his species he was kindly disposed and respectful. Directions were given him to drive to a friend's house. He said that his horse was too tired, but if I were willing, he had another "at his place," where he would drive me and change.

Quite willing, or rather too weary to assert any authority, so on we rumbled and rattled almost twice the distance I was first bound, changed one skeleton for another, and started again for my friend's house. At last the blessed haven was reached, but the sight of a new face to my summons at the door made my heart sink. She had "moved yesterday."

"Drive to Miss G.'s house," was my next direction, intending to throw myself upon her hospitality and charity for the night, for we were out of the way of all hotels.

The same result on application. Had all Richmond moved? The fresh air, and the necessity for exertion in this novel position had routed my head-ache, and now gave me courage to make a proposition I hadn't dared to make before.

"Could not you drive me to the hospital on the hill?" was my demand made in most ingratiating tones.

The old man untied the rag from off his head, and smoothed it on his knee by way of ironing out the creases and assisting reflection; replaced it, taking up the reins again before he answered, for we were now at a stand-still at the Broad Street hill.

"Missis," said he solemnly, "de way it is long, and de bridges dey is rotten; but ef you is not afeared to dribe ober dem by you-self, and let me git out, and pay me ten dollars, de ole hoss might be consarned to go up dis yere hill."

The bargain was struck, and the hospital reached after midnight. The key of my apartments sent for, when the duplicate hair that at last broke the camel's back was laid upon mine.

"Miss G. had taken it with her."

"Bring a carpenter," I cried desperately; "and tell him to get a sledge-hammer and knock down, or in, anything that will let me get into the place. I *must* have rest."

The door was broken open; a fire was kindled; a delicious piece of cold hard cornbread found and devoured, and when the warm covering of the first bed I had slept in for ten days was drawn around me, all the troubles of a hard world melted away, and the only real happiness on earth, entire exemption from mental and bodily pain, took possession of me.

Fourteen

I noticed on my return a great difference in the means of living between Virginia and the Gulf States. Even in the most wealthy and luxurious houses in Richmond, former everyday comforts had about this time become luxuries, and had been dispensed with earlier in the war. Farther south, they still received from Nassau what they needed, always running the risks of losing the cargoes of the blockade-runners, therefore duplicating orders. Tea and coffee were first given up at the capital, then many used corn flour, —wheat was so high. Gradually butter disappeared from the breakfast table, and brown sugar when it reached twenty dollars a pound shared the same fate. But no such economy appeared necessary where I had been. The air of the people in the cars and around the railroad stations was hopeful in the extreme. There was no doubt expressed even at this late day, the November of 1864, as to the ultimate success of the Southern cause.

Their hospitals though did not compare with those I had left in Virginia, either in arrangement, cleanliness or attendance. Even as early as 1862 the matrons' places there had been filled by ladies of education and refinement; but this with a few exceptions had been the rule in Virginia only, and such supervision made a marked difference, as may be supposed.

During my absence, the greater portion of the patients I had left a month previously had either recovered and left, or died, so that it was awkward to resume my duties among strangers. A few days' visiting rectified this however. The happiest welcome I got was from Miss G., who resigned the key of the liquor closet with a sigh which spoke volumes. From what could be gathered, she had been equal to the occasion, and knowing the hardship of her dragonship I did not press her strenuously upon points connected with it.

The health of the army was now so good, that except when the wounded were sent in, we were comparatively idle. That terrible scourge, pneumonia, so prevalent early in the war, and so fatal in its typhoid form, had almost disappeared. The men had become accustomed and inured to exposure. Christmas passed pleasantly. The hospital fund (from the great depreciation of the money) being too small to allow us to make much festive preparation, the ladies of the city drove out in carriages and ambulances laden with good things. The previous years we had been enabled to give out of the expenditure of our own funds a bowl of eggnogg and a slice of cake, for lunch, to every man in the hospital, as well as his portion of turkey and oysters for dinner; but times were more stringent now.

Soon after New Year, 1865, some members of the committee on hospital affairs called to see me, desirous of getting some information regarding the use or abuse of liquor, before the bill for the appropriations for the coming year would be introduced. There were doubts afloat as to whether the benefit conferred upon the patients by the use of stimulants counterbalanced the evil effects they produced on the surgeons, who were in the habit of making use of them when they could get them.

The problem was difficult to solve. A case in point had lately come under my observation. A man had been brought into our hospital with a crushed ankle, the cars having run over it. He had been attended to, and the leg put in splints before we had received him, so as he was still heavy and drowsy, possibly from some anodyne administered, the surgeon in attendance ordered him to be left undisturbed. The nurse in a few hours came to me to say that the man was suffering intensely. He had a burning fever, and complained of the fellow leg instead of the injured one. The natural idea of sympathy occurred, and a sedative given which failed in producing any effect. I determined to look at it in spite of orders, his sufferings appearing so great, and finding the foot and leg above and below the splint perfectly well, the thought of examining the fellow leg suggested itself. It was a most shocking sight—swollen, inflamed and purple—the drunken surgeon had set the wrong leg! The pain induced low fever, which eventually assumed a typhoid form, and the man died. With this instance fresh in my memory I hesitated to give any opinion in favor, and yet felt we could not manage without the liquor. However, the appropriation was made.

This poor fellow was the most dependent patient I ever had, and though entirely uneducated, won his way to my sympathies by his entire helplessness and belief in the efficacy of my care and advice. No surgeon in the hospital could persuade him to swallow anything in the shape of food unless I sanctioned the order, and a few kindly words, or an encouraging nod would satisfy and please him. His ideas of luxuries were curious, and his answer to my daily inquiries of what he could fancy for food, was invariably the same—he would like some "scribbled eggs and flitters." This order was complied with three times daily, until the doctor prescribed stronger food and though many dainties were substituted, he still called them by the same name, leading me to suppose that "scribbled eggs and flitters" was his generic term for food. I made him some jelly, Confederate jelly—with the substitution of whiskey for Madeira wine, and citric acid for lemons, but he said "he did not like it, there was no chewing on it," and "it all went, he did not know where!" so I gave up trying to tempt his palate.

When whole wards would be emptied of their occupants, in compliance with changes made to suit certain views of the surgical department, and strangers put in, I would always feel a great repugnance to visiting them. But when the change became gradual, by the convalescents, in twos or threes or half-dozens, being exchanged for invalids, there would always be enough men left to whom I was known, to make me feel at home, and to inform the newcomers why I came among them, and what my duties were. I now found my hospital filled with strangers. They were not so considerate as my old friends had been, and looked rather with suspicion upon my daily visits. One man amused me particularly by keeping a portion of his food every day for my special and agreeable inspection, as he thought, and my particular annoyance, as I felt. A specimen of everything he thought unpalatable was deposited under his pillow, to await my arrival, and the greeting invariably given me was:

"Do you call that good bread?"

"Well no, not very good; but the flour is very dark and musty."

Another day he would draw out a handful of dry rice.

"Do you call *that* properly boiled?"

"That is the way we boil rice in Carolina. Each grain must be separated."

"Well! I won't eat mine boiled that way."

And so on through all the details of his food. Somebody he felt was responsible, and unfortunately he determined that I should be the scapegoat. His companion who lay by his side was even more disagreeable than he was. Being a terrible pickle consumer, he indulged in such extreme dissipation in that luxury that a check had to be put upon his appetite. He attacked me upon this grievance the first chance he found, and listened scornfully to my remarks that pickles were luxuries to be eaten sparingly and used carefully. "Perhaps," he said at last, "we would have more pickles if you had fewer new dresses." There was no doubt that I wore a new homespun dress, but what connection it had with the pickles was rather mysterious. However, that afternoon came a formal apology, written in quite an elegant style, and signed by every man in the ward, except the pickle man, in which the fault of this cruel speech was laid upon the bad whiskey.

FIFTEEN

*A*ll this winter of '64, the city had been unusually gay. Besides parties, private theatricals and tableaux were constantly exhibited. Wise and thoughtful men disapproved openly of this mad gayety. There was certainly a painful discrepancy between the excitement of dancing and the rumble of ambulances that could be heard in the momentary lull of the music, carrying the wounded to the different hospitals. Young men advocated this state of affairs, arguing that after the fatigues and dangers of a campaign in the field, some relaxation was necessary on their visits to the capital.

To thinking people this recklessness was ominous; and by the end of February, 1865, it began to be felt by them that all was not as safe as it was supposed to be. The incessant moving of troops through the city from one point to another proved weakness, and the scarcity of rations issued told a painful tale. People rated the inefficiency of the commissary department, and predicted that a change in its administration would make all right. Soon afterwards the truth was told me in confidence and under promise of strict secrecy. Richmond would be evacuated in a month or six weeks. The time might be lengthened or shortened, but the fact was established.

Then came the packing up, quietly but surely, of the different departments. Requisitions on the medical purveyor were returned unfilled, and an order from the surgeon-general required that herbs instead of licensed medicines should be used in the hospitals. There was a great deal of merriment elicited from the "yarb teas," drawn during this time by the surgeons; few knowing the sad cause of their substitution. My mind had been very unsettled as to my course of action in view of the impending crash, but my duty prompted me to remain with my sick, on the ground that no general ever deserts his troops. But to be left by all my friends to meet the dangers and privations of an invested city, among antagonistic influences, with the prospect of being turned out of my office the next day after the surrender, was not a cheering one. Even my home would no longer be open to me; for staying with a cabinet minister, he would leave with the government. I was spared the necessity of decision by the sudden attack of General Grant, and the breaking of the Confederate lines, and before there was time to think at all, the government and all its train had vanished.

~

On the 2nd of April, 1865, while the congregation of Dr. Charles Minnegarode's church in Richmond were listening to his Sunday sermon, a
messenger entered and handed a telegram to Mr. Davis, then president of
the Confederate States, who rose immediately, and without any visible
signs of agitation or surprise, left the church. No alarm was exhibited by
the congregation, though several members of the president's staff followed
him, till Dr. Minnegarode brought the service to an abrupt close, and
informed his startled flock that the city would be evacuated shortly, and
they would only exercise a proper degree of prudence by going home
immediately, and preparing for the event. This announcement, although
coming from such a reliable source, hardly availed to convince the Virginians that their beloved capital, assailed so often, defended so bravely, surrounded by fortifications on which the engineering talents of their best
officers had been expended, was to be capitulated. Some months before, a
small number admitted behind the veil of the temple had been apprised
that the sacrifice was to be accomplished; that General Lee had again and
again urged Mr. Davis to yield this Mecca of his heart to the interests of the
Confederacy, and resign a city which required an army to hold it, and pick-
ets to be posted from thirty to forty miles around it, weakening his depleted
army; and again and again had the iron will triumphed, and the foe, beaten
and discomfited, retired for fresh combinations and fresh troops

But the hour had come, and the evacuation was only a question of time.
Day and night had the whistle of cars proved to the anxious people that
brigades were being moved to strengthen this point or defend that; and
no one was able to say exactly where any portion of the army of Virginia
was stationed. That Grant would make an effort to strike the Southside
railroad—the main artery for the conveyance of food to the city—every
one *knew;* and that General Lee would be able to meet the effort and check
it, everybody *hoped,* and while this hope lasted there was no panic.

The telegram which reached Mr. Davis that Sunday morning, was to the
effect that the enemy *had* struck, and on the weakest point of the Confederate lines. It told him to be prepared in event of the repulse failing. Two
hours after came the fatal news that Grant had forced his way through,
and that the city must instantly be evacuated. What is meant by that
simple sentence "evacuation of the city" but few can imagine who have not
experienced it.

The officials of the various departments hurried to their offices, speedily packing up everything connected with the government. The quartermaster's and commissary's stores were thrown open and thousands of the half-starved and half-clad people of Richmond rushed to the scene.

Delicate women tottered under the weight of hams, bags of coffee, flour and sugar. Invalided officers carried away articles of unaccustomed luxury for sick wives and children at home. Every vehicle was in requisition, commanding fabulous remuneration, and gold or silver the only currency accepted. The immense concourse of government employes, speculators, gamblers, strangers, pleasure and profit lovers of all kinds that had been attached to that great center, the Capital, were "packing," while those who had determined to stay and await the chances of war, tried to look calmly on, and draw courage from their faith in the justness of their cause.

The wives and families of Mr. Davis and his cabinet had been sent away some weeks previously, so that no provision had been made for the transportation of any particular class of people. All the cars that could be collected were at the Fredericksburg depot, and by 3 o'clock P.M. the trains commenced to move. The scene at the station was of indescribable confusion. No one could afford to abandon any article of wear or household use, when going where they knew that nothing could be replaced. Baggage was as valuable as life, and life was represented there by wounded and sick officers and men, helpless women and children, for all who could be with the army were at their post.

Hour after hour fled and still the work went on. The streets were strewn with torn papers, records and documents too burdensome to carry away, too important to be left for inspection, and people still thronged the thoroughfares, loaded with stores until then hoarded by the government and sutler shops.

The scream and rumble of the cars never ceased all that weary night, and was perhaps the most painful sound to those left behind, for all the rest of the city seemed flying; but while the center of Richmond was in the wildest confusion, so sudden had been the shock that the suburbs were quiet and even ignorant of the scenes enacting in the heart of the city. Events crowded so rapidly upon each other that no one had time to spread reports.

There was no change in the appearance of the surroundings till near midnight, when the school-ship, the *Patrick Henry,* formerly the old United States ship *Yorktown,* was fired at the wharf at Rocketts (the extreme eastern end of the city). The blowing up of her magazine seemed the signal for the work of destruction to commence. Explosions followed from all points. The warehouses and tobacco manufactories were fired, communicating the flames to the adjacent houses and shops, and soon Main Street was in a blaze. The armory, not intended to be burnt, either caught accidentally or was fired by mistake; the shells exploding and filling the air with hissing sounds of horror, menacing the people in every direction. Colonel [Josiah] Gorgas had endeavored to spike or destroy them by rolling them into the canal, and but for this precaution with the largest, the city would have been almost leveled to the dust.

No one slept during that night of horror, for added to the present scenes were the anticipations of what the morrow would bring forth. Daylight dawned upon a wreck of destruction and desolation. From the highest point of Church hill and Libby hill, the eye could range over the whole extent of city and country—the fire had not abated, and the burning bridges were adding their flame and smoke to the scene. A single faint explosion could be heard from the distance at long intervals, but the *Patrick Henry* was low to the water's edge and Drewry but a column of smoke. The whistle of the cars and the rushing of the laden trains still continued—they had never ceased—and the clouds hung low and draped the scene as morning advanced.

SIXTEEN

*B*efore the sun had risen, two carriages rolled along Main Street, and passed through Rocketts just under Chimborazo hospital, carrying the mayor and corporation towards the Federal lines, to deliver the keys of the city, and half an hour afterwards, over to the east, a single Federal blue-jacket rose above the hill, standing transfixed with astonishment at what he saw. Another and another sprang up as if out of the earth, but still all remained quiet. About seven o'clock, there fell upon the ear the steady clatter of horses' hoofs, and winding around Rocketts, close under Chimborazo hill, came a small and compact body of Federal cavalrymen, on horses in splendid condition, riding closely and steadily along. They were well mounted, well accoutered, well fed—a rare sight in Southern streets,—the advance of that vaunted army that for four years had so hopelessly knocked at the gates of the Southern Confederacy.

They were some distance in advance of the infantry who followed, quite as well appointed and accoutered as the cavalry. Company after company, regiment after regiment, battalion after battalion, and brigade after brigade, they poured into the doomed city—an endless stream. One detachment separated from the main body and marching to Battery No. 2, raised the United States flag, their band playing the Star Spangled Banner. There they stacked their arms. The rest marched along Main street through fire and smoke, over burning fragments of buildings, emerging at times like a phantom army when the wind lifted the dark clouds; while the colored population shouted and cheered them on their way.

Before three hours had elapsed, the troops had been quartered and were inspecting the city. They swarmed in every highway and byway, rose out of gullies, appeared on the top of hills, emerged from narrow lanes, and skirted around low fences. There was hardly a spot in Richmond not occupied by a blue coat, but they were orderly, quiet and respectful. Thoroughly disciplined, warned not to give offense by look or act, they did not speak to any one unless first addressed; and though the women of the South contrasted with sickness of heart the difference between this splendidly-equipped army, and the war-worn, wasted aspect of their own defenders, they were grateful for the consideration shown them; and if they remained in their sad homes, with closed doors and windows, or walked the streets with averted eyes and veiled faces, it was that they could not bear the presence of invaders, even under the most favorable circumstances.

Before the day was over, the public buildings were occupied by the enemy, and the minds of the citizens relieved from all fear of molestation. The hospitals were attended to, the ladies being still allowed to nurse and care for their own wounded; but rations could not be drawn yet, the obstructions in the James river preventing the transports from coming up to the city. In a few days they arrived, and food was issued to those in need. It had been a matter of pride among the Southerners to boast that they had never seen a greenback, so the entrance of the Federal army had thus found them entirely unprepared with gold and silver currency. People who had boxes of Confederate money and were wealthy the day previously, looked around in vain for wherewithal to buy a loaf of bread. Strange exchanges were made on the street of tea and coffee, flour and bacon. Those who were fortunate in having a stock of household necessaries were generous in the extreme to their less wealthy neighbors, but the destitution was terrible. The sanitary commission shops were opened, and commissioners appointed by the Federals to visit among the people and distribute orders to draw rations, but to effect this, after receiving tickets, required so many appeals to different officials, that decent people gave up the effort. Besides, the musty cornmeal and strong cod-fish were not appreciated by fastidious stomachs—few gently nurtured could relish such unfamiliar food.

But there was no assimilation between the invaders and invaded. In the daily newspaper a notice had appeared that the military bands would play in the beautiful capital grounds every afternoon, but when the appointed hour arrived, except the Federal officers, musicians and soldiers, not a white face was to be seen. The negroes crowded every bench and path. The next week another notice was issued that the colored population would not be admitted; and then the absence of everything and anything feminine was appalling. The entertainers went alone to their own entertainment. The third week still another notice appeared: "colored nurses were to be admitted with their white charges," and lo! each fortunate white baby received the cherished care of a dozen finely-dressed black ladies, the only drawback being that in two or three days the music ceased altogether, the entertainers feeling at last the ingratitude of the subjugated people.

Despite their courtesy of manner, for however despotic the acts, the Federal authorities maintained a respectful manner—the newcomers made no advance towards fraternity. They spoke openly and warmly of their sympathy with the sufferings of the South, but committed and advocated acts that the hearers could not recognize as "military necessities." Bravely-dressed Federal officers met their former old class-mates from colleges and military institutions and inquired after the relatives to whose houses they had ever been welcome in days of yore, expressing a desire to "call and see them," while the vacant chairs, rendered vacant by Federal bullets, stood by the hearth of the widow and bereaved mother. They could not be made to understand that their presence was painful. There were few men in the city at this time; but the women of the South still fought their battle for them: fought it resentfully, calmly, but silently! Clad in their mourning garments, overcome but hardly subdued, they sat within their desolate homes, or if compelled to leave that shelter went on their errands to church or hospital with veiled faces and swift steps. By no sign or act did the possessors of their fair city know that they were even conscious of their presence. If they looked in their faces they saw them not: they might have supposed themselves a phantom army. There was no stepping aside with affectation to avoid the contact of dress, no feigned humility in giving the inside of the walk: they simply totally ignored their presence.

Two particular characteristics followed the army in possession—the circus and booths for the temporary accommodation of itinerant venders. The small speculators must have supposed that there were no means of cooking left in the city, from the quantity of canned edibles they offered for sale. They inundated Richmond with pictorial canisters at exorbitant prices, which no one had money to buy. Whether the supply of greenbacks was scant, or the people were not disposed to trade with the new-comers, they had no customers.

In a few days steamboats had made their way to the wharves, though the obstructions still defied the ironclads, and crowds of curious strangers thronged the pavements, while squads of mounted male pleasure-seekers scoured the streets. Gayly-dressed women began to pour in also, with looped-up skirts, very large feet, and a great preponderance of spectacles. The Richmond women sitting by desolated firesides were astonished by the arrival of former friends, sometimes people moving in the best classes of society, who had the bad taste to make a pleasure trip to the mourning city, calling upon their heart-broken friends of happier days in all the finery of the newest New York fashions, and in some instances forgiving their entertainers the manifold sins of the last four years in formal and set terms.

From the hill on which my hospital was built, I had sat all the weary Sunday of the evacuation, watching the turmoil, and bidding friends adieu, for even till noon many had been unconscious of the events that were transpiring, and now when they had all departed, as night set in, I wrapped my blanket-shawl around me, and watched below me all that I have here narrated. Then I walked through my wards and found them comparatively empty. Every man who could crawl had tried to escape a Northern prison. Beds in which paralyzed, rheumatic, and helpless patients had laid for months were empty. The miracles of the New Testament had been re-enacted. The lame, the halt, and the blind had been cured. Those who were compelled to remain were almost wild at being left in what would be the enemy's lines the next day; for in many instances they had been exchanged prisoners only a short time before. I gave all the comfort I could, and with some difficulty their supper also, for my detailed nurses had gone with General Lee's army, and my black cooks had deserted me.

On Monday morning, the day after the evacuation, the first blue uniforms appeared at our quarters—three surgeons inspecting the hospital. As our surgeon was with them, there must have been an amicable understanding. One of our divisions was required for use by the newcomers, cleared out for them, and their patients laid by the side of our own sick so that we shared with them, as my own commissary stores were still well supplied. Three days afterwards an order came to transfer my old patients to Camp Jackson. I protested bitterly against this, as they were not in a fit state for removal, so they remained unmolested. To them I devoted my time, for our surgeons had either then left or received orders to discontinue their labors.

Towards evening the place was deserted. Miss G. had remained up to this time with me, but her mother requiring her presence in the city, she left at sunset, and after I had gone through all my wards, I returned to my dear little sitting-room, endeared by retrospection, and the consciousness that my labors were nearly over, but had been (as far as regarded results) in vain!

SEVENTEEN

The federal authorities had as yet posted no guards around, and as our own had been withdrawn, or rather had left, being under no control or direction, not a sound broke the stillness of the sad night. Exhausted with all the exciting events of the day, it was not to be wondered at that I soon fell asleep heavily and dreamlessly, to be awakened in an hour by the crash of an adjoining door, and passing into my pantry from whence the sound proceeded I came upon a group of men, who had burst the entrance opening upon the back premises. As my eye traveled from face to face, I recognized them as a set of "hospital rats" whom I had never been able to get rid of, for if sent to the field one week, they would be sure to be back the next, on some trifling pretext of sickness or disability. The ringleader was an old enemy, who had stored up many a grievance against me, but my acts of kindness to his sickly wife naturally made me suppose his wrath had been disarmed. He acted on this occasion as spokesman, and the trouble was the old one. Thirty gallons of whiskey had been sent to me the day before the evacuation, and they wanted it.

"We have come for the whiskey!"

"You cannot, and shall not have it."

"It does not belong to you."

"It is in my charge, and I intend to keep it. Go out of my pantry; you are all drunk."

"Boys!" he said, "pick up that barrel and carry it down the hill. I will attend to *her!*"

But the habit of obedience of four years still had its effect on the boys, for all the movement they made was in a retrograde direction.

"Wilson," I said, "you have been in this hospital a long time. Do you think from what you know of me that the whiskey can be taken without my consent?"

He became very insolent.

"Stop that talk; your great friends have all gone, and we won't stand that now. Move out of the way!"

He advanced towards the barrel, and so did I, only being in the inside, I interposed between him and the object of contention. The fierce temper blazed up in his face, and catching me roughly by the shoulder, he called me a name that a decent woman seldom hears and even a wicked one resents. But I had a little friend, which usually reposed quietly on the shelf, but had been removed to my pocket in the last twenty-four hours, more from a sense of protection than from any idea that it would be called into active service; so before he had time to push me one inch from my position, or to see what kind of an ally was in my hand, that sharp click, a sound so signifi- cant and so different from any other, struck upon his ear, and sent him back amidst his friends, pale and shaken.

"You had better leave," I said, composedly (for I felt in my feminine soul that although I was near enough to pinch his nose, that I had missed him), "for if *one* bullet is lost, there are five more ready, and the room is too small for even a woman to miss six times."

There was a conference held at the shattered door, resulting in an agreement to leave, but he shook his fist wrathfully at my small pop-gun.

"You think yourself very brave now, but wait an hour; perhaps others may have pistols too, and you won't have it entirely your way after all."

My first act was to take the head of one of the flour barrels and nail it across the door as tightly as I could, with a two-pound weight for a ham- mer, and then, warm with triumph and victory gained, I sat down by my whiskey barrel and felt the affection we all bestow on what we have cher- ished, fought for, and defended successfully; then putting a candle, a box of matches, and a pistol within reach of my hand, I went to sleep, never wak- ing until late in the morning, having heard nothing more of my visitors.

The next day the steward informed me that our stores had been taken possession of by the Federal authorities, so we could not draw the neces- sary rations. The surgeons had all left; therefore I prepared for a visit to headquarters, by donning my full-dress toilette: boots of untanned leather, tied with thongs; a Georgia woven homespun dress in black and white blocks—the white, cotton yarn, the black, an old silk, washed, scraped with broken glass into pulp, and then carded and spun (it was an elegant thing); white cuffs and collar of bleached homespun, and a hat plaited of the rye straw picked from the field back of us, dyed black with walnut juice, a shoe- string for ribbon to encircle it; and knitted worsted gloves of three shades of green—the darkest bottle shade being around the wrist, while the color tapered to the loveliest blossom of the pea at the finger-tips. The style of the make was Confederate.

Thus splendidly equipped I walked to Dr. M.'s office, now Federal head-quarters, and making my way through a crowd of blue coats, accosted the principal figure seated there, with a stern and warlike demand for food, and a curt inquiry whether it was their intention to starve their captured sick. He was very polite, laid the blame on the obstructions in the river, which prevented their transports getting up. I requested that as such was the case I might be allowed to reclaim my ambulance, now under their lock and key, in order to take some coffee then in my possession to the city and exchange it for animal food. It had been saved from rations formerly drawn, and donations given. He wished to know why it had not been turned over to the U. S. government, but did not press the point as I was not communica-tive, and gave me the necessary order for the vehicle. Then polite conver-sation commenced.

"Was I a native of Virginia?"

"No; I was a South Carolinian, who had gone to Virginia at the com-mencement of the war to try and aid in alleviating the sufferings and pri-vations of the hospitals."

"He had lost a brother in South Carolina."

"It was the fate of war. Self-preservation was the first law of nature. As a soldier he must recognize defense of one's native soil."

"He regretted the present state of scarcity, for he could see in the pale faces and pinched features of the Richmond women, how much they had suffered during the war."

I retorted quickly this wound to both patriotism and vanity. He meant to be polite, but that he was unlucky was shown by my answer.

"If my features were pinched, and my face pale, it was not caused by privations under the Confederacy, but the anguish consequent upon our failure."

But his kindness had once again put my ambulance under my control, and placing a bag of coffee and a demijohn of whiskey in it, I assumed the reins, having no driver, and went to market. The expedition was successful, as I returned shortly with a live calf, for which I had exchanged them, and which summoned every one within hearing by its bellowing. I had quite won the heart of the Vermonter who had been sentry at my door, and though patriotic souls may not believe me, he paid me many compliments at the expense of the granite ladies of his State. The compliments were sincere, as he refused the drink of whiskey my gratitude offered him.

My next visit was to the commissary department of my hospital in search of sugar. Two Federal guards were in charge, but they simply stared with astonishment as I put aside their bayonets and unlocked the door of the place with my pass-key, filled my basket, with an explanation to them that I could be arrested whenever wanted at my quarters.

After this no one opposed my erratic movements, the new-comers ignoring me. No explanation was ever given to me, why I was allowed to come and go, nurse my men and feed them with all I could take or steal. All I ever gathered was from one of our errand-boys, who had fraternized with a Yankee sutler, who told him confidentially that the Federal surgeon in charge thought that woman in black had better go home, and added on his own responsibility, "He's awful afraid of her."

Away I was compelled to go at last, for my sick were removed to another hospital, where I still attended to them. There congregated the ladies of the neighborhood, bringing what delicacies they could gather, and nursing indiscriminately any patient who needed care. This continued till all the sick were either convalescent or dead, and at last my vocation was gone, and not one invalid left to give me a pretext for daily occupation.

And now when the absorbing duties of the last years no longer demanded my whole thoughts and attention, the difficulties of my own position forced themselves upon my mind. Whatever food had been provided for the sick since the Federal occupation had served for my small needs, but when my duties ceased I found myself with a box full of Confederate money and a sil-ver ten-cent piece; perhaps a Confederate *gage d'amitie;* which puzzled me how to expend. It was all I had for a support, so I bought a box of matches and five cocoa-nut cakes. The wisdom of the purchase there is no need of defending. Should any one ever be in a strange country where the currency of which he is possessed is valueless, and ten cents be his only available funds, perhaps he may be able to judge of the difficulty of expending it with judgment.

But of what importance was the fact that I was houseless, homeless and moneyless, in Richmond, the heart of Virginia? Who ever wanted for aught that kind hearts, generous hands or noble hospitality could supply, that it was not there offered without even the shadow of a patronage that could have made it distasteful? What women were ever so refined in feeling and so unaffected in manner; so willing to share all that wealth gives, and so little infected with the pride of purse that bestows that power? It was difficult to hide one's needs from them; they found them out and ministered to them with their quiet simplicity and the innate nobility which gave to their generosity the coloring of a favor received; not conferred.

I laughed carelessly and openly at the disregard shown by myself for the future, when every one who had remained in Richmond, apparently had laid aside stores for daily food, but they detected with quick sympathy the hollowness of the mirth, and each day at every hour of breakfast, dinner and supper, would come to me a waiter, borne by the neat little Virginia maid (in her white apron), filled with ten times the quantity of food I could consume, packed carefully on. Sometimes boxes would be left at my door, with packages of tea, coffee, sugar and ham, or chicken, and no clue given to the thoughtful and kind donor.

Would that I could do more than thank the dear friends who made my life for four years so happy and contented; who never made me feel by word or act, that my self-imposed occupation was otherwise than one which would ennoble any woman. If ever any aid was given through my own exertions, or any labor rendered effective by me for the good of the South—if any sick soldier ever benefited by my happy face or pleasant smiles at his bedside, or death was ever soothed by gentle words of hope and tender care, such results were only owing to the cheering encouragement I received from them. They were gentle-women in every sense of the word, and though they might not have remembered that *"noblesse oblige"* they felt and acted up to the motto in every act of their lives. My only wish was to live and die among them, growing each day better from contact with their gentle, kindly sympathies and heroic hearts.

It may never be in my power to do more than offer my heartfelt thanks, which may reach their once happy homes; and in closing these simple reminiscences of hospital experience, let me beg them to believe that whatever kindness my limited powers have conferred on the noble soldiers of their state, has been repaid tenfold, leaving me with an eternal, but grateful obligation.

There is one subject connected with hospitals on which a few words should be said—the distasteful one that a woman must lose a certain amount of delicacy and reticence in filling any office in them. How can this be? There is no unpleasant exposure under proper arrangements, and if even there be, the circumstances which surround a wounded man, far from friends and home, suffering in a holy cause and dependent upon a woman for help, care and sympathy, hallow and clear the atmosphere in which she labors. That woman must indeed be hard and gross, who lets one material thought lessen her efficiency. In the midst of suffering and death, hoping with those almost beyond hope in this world; praying by the bedside of the lonely and heart-stricken; closing the eyes of boys hardly old enough to realize man's sorrows, much less suffer by man's fierce hate, a woman *must* soar beyond the conventional modesty considered correct under different circumstances.

If the ordeal does not chasten and purify her nature, if the contemplation of suffering and endurance does not make her wiser and better, and if the daily fire through which she passes does not draw from her nature the sweet fragrance of benevolence, charity, and love,—then, indeed a hospital has been no fit place for her!

∿

THE END.

NOTES

1. For biographical information on Pember and her family, see the excellent account in Robert N. Rosen, *The Jewish Confederates* (Columbia: University of South Carolina Press, 2000), 280–303, and Bell Wiley's introduction to his edition of Phoebe Yates Pember, *A Southern Woman's Story: Life in Confederate Richmond* (Jackson, Tenn.: McCowat-Mercer Press, 1959), 1–19. Wiley's edition included nine of Pember's wartime letters found in the manuscripts collections of the Southern Historical Collection, University of North Carolina, Chapel Hill, and the Library of Congress.

2. For later descriptions of Pember's social activities, see Thomas Cooper DeLeon, *Belles, Beaux and Brains of the 60's* (New York: G. W. Dillingham Company, 1907), 229–231.

3. Pember (1959), 185.

4. Ibid., 156.

5. Ibid., 169–70.

6. One contemporary recalled her as a refined, attractive, and strong woman who defiantly stood her ground against anyone (DeLeon, *Belles, Beaux, and Brains of the 60's,* 385).

7. On the wartime conversion of Jews, see Lauren F. Winner, "Taking Up the Cross: Conversion among Black and White Jews in the Civil War South," in *Southern Families at War: Loyalty and Conflict in the Civil War South,* ed. Catherine Clinton (New York: Oxford University Press, 2000), 193–207.

8. Pember (1959), 168.

9. Phoebe Pember, "Confederate Nurse," was also immortalized on a stamp issued by the U.S. Postal Service in 1995 as part of a series to commemorate various Civil War figures and events.

10. "Reminiscences of a Southern Hospital. By its Matron," parts 1–4, *Cosmopolite* 1 (January 1866): 70–88; (February 1866): 203–15; (March 1866): 296–309; (April 1866): 348–69.

11. In 1991, Broadfoot Publishing Company reprinted the Wiley edition, and Mockingbird Books published a mass market paperback edition.

12. Mary Elizabeth Massey, *Bonnet Brigades* (New York: Alfred A. Knopf, 1966), 48, 57–58, 88, 188, 255; George C. Rable, *Civil Wars: Women and the Crisis of Southern Nationalism* (Urbana: University of Illinois Press, 1989), 123, 125–27, 155, 197–198. Drew Gilpin Faust has made the point that in many ways Phoebe Pember was more a "hospital administrator" than a nurse (*Mothers of Invention: Women of the Slaveholding South in the American Civil War* [Chapel Hill: University of North Carolina Press, 1996], 98–102).